Time With GOD In Finding Inner Peace

LALONIE BOWEN

BALBOA
PRESS
A DIVISION OF HAY HOUSE

Balboa Press books may be ordered through booksellers or by contacting:

Balboa Press
A Division of Hay House
1663 Liberty Drive
Bloomington, IN 47403
www.balboapress.com
1 (877) 407-4847

Because of the dynamic nature of the Internet, any web addresses or links contained in
this book may have changed since publication and may no longer be valid. The views
expressed in this work are solely those of the author and do not necessarily reflect the
views of the publisher, and the publisher hereby disclaims any responsibility for them.

The author of this book does not dispense medical advice or prescribe the use
of any technique as a form of treatment for physical, emotional, or medical
problems without the advice of a physician, either directly or indirectly. The
intent of the author is only to offer information of a general nature to help you
in your quest for emotional and spiritual well-being. In the event you use any
of the information in this book for yourself, which is your constitutional right,
the author and the publisher assume no responsibility for your actions.

Any people depicted in stock imagery provided by Thinkstock are models,
and such images are being used for illustrative purposes only.
Certain stock imagery © Thinkstock.

Print information available on the last page.

ISBN: 978-1-5043-6255-9 (sc)
ISBN: 978-1-5043-6257-3 (hc)
ISBN: 978-1-5043-6256-6 (e)

Library of Congress Control Number: 2016911824

Balboa Press rev. date: 08/10/2016

TABLE OF CONTENTS

INTRODUCTION

I have felt so called to write this book on spending time in prayer with God. It is almost as though God is taking me by the reins and moving me along this journey of writing this book. I have written this book in order to uplift and inspire people along their life path so they too can find the inner peace I found in spending quality time with God. Many times we go through life feeling as though there is something missing in our lives, and so we begin searching and seeking out what it is we need. When I began that process of seeking, I found that the only lack I had in my life was the gift of Jesus and God, and once I began that journey of a one on one relationship with God, then my life changed in a dramatic and wonderful way, and this is what I want for you too.

I hope this book makes a real difference in your life as it did mine when I began my daily prayer time with God. I feel in my heart that we all need the love of God. To know each and everyday as we make our way through this life that there is one constant knowledge we can have, and that is that God loves us so very, very much, more than we could ever even imagine. To know that no matter what is going on in our lives that we are never alone, that God is always with us every single day of our lives. Always loving us, and always supporting us and never leaving our side. It is so important to understand that God lives inside your heart, holding your hand and embracing you!

This book teaches you the importance of daily prayer time, and the value of honoring and praising God every single day. The one on one relationship you can build with God by spending time in prayer with HIM everyday, and how it will make such a difference in your life. HE is always there, and always listening to your words and what is in your heart. It can bring you more joy and more peace and more love than you have ever known.

My wish is for you to really get to know Jesus and God, and to show you how to bring them into your world, so you can see for yourself the change and the difference and the great impact it can have on your life.

My desire is for you to have the best life possible, and I pray this book will enlighten you and bring you joy and peace, love and happiness as I hope you can feel what I have experienced from words on the pages.

I hope this book helps make a difference in your life, and brings inspiration and hope into your soul, and creates a joyful look at how your life can be with Jesus and God as a part of your daily existence.

The most important piece of information to relay to you is to let you know that more than anything Jesus and God just want to be a part of your life. They really want to hear from you, and want you to speak to them in prayer and conversation, and to share your wants and your desires, and they want to know what worries or concerns you have so they can help you in your life journey. I hope you will give of yourself to God, as HE is waiting patiently to hear from you. Be patient with God, as HE answers our prayers, not in our time frame, but in HIS time, as HE is always working behind the scenes for good things to come into our lives.

Always remember, you are loved unconditionally by God, as you are HIS child, and HE wants nothing but the very best for you! God Bless You!!

DEDICATION

I am dedicating this book in honor of my friend Linda Shaffner! Linda and I were best friends for 33 years. We met in our late 20's as young Moms, and we would get together for coffee and cinnamon rolls in a Moms group, and we became instant friends. Never in my life have I become a friend so fast with anyone ever before. It was amazing how we just clicked so quickly as friends. We went through a lot in our personal lives together, always loving and supporting each other.

Linda believed in me as a writer way back then, and always encouraged me and supported me in my endeavor to become an author. She was always coming up with ideas of what I could write about, as she believed in me wholeheartedly and had such strong faith in me as a writer. I entered a writing contest in my late 30's, and out of 250 entries, they chose the top 25 to publish in a newspaper, and my story was one of the chosen ones. I couldn't believe it! What a great honor it was for me, especially as my very first venture in writing. Linda bought me a statue of a deer and an angel, representing the story I had submitted. Today I still have that statue, and will keep it always as the reminder of her and her faith and her love for me.

My friend Linda passed away in her late 50's. I couldn't believe she was gone from my life. Even though she had moved to another town we still made sure we got together and we talked on the phone a lot and sent many emails back and forth. I gave the Eulogy at Linda's funeral. It was so important for me to make sure everyone knew what a wonderful person she was. She was a loving and caring nurse to many. She was compassionate as a nurse and gave her all to every patient she cared for. She was a loving Mom to her two daughters, Lisa and Angela, and she adored her grandchildren!!

Linda and I could finish each other's sentences, and we loved being together, and we laughed so much. So many great memories I have of her, and so many great moments we had together. I will never forget her. She lives in my heart. She is a part of me, and will always be. I miss her everyday! I treasure our times we had together, and I feel her presence around me. I thank God for bringing her into my life, as she was such a gift to me for all of the years we had.

I love you Linda, and I thank you for your friendship, your love, your care, and I am so grateful for the blessing of you. This book is for you Linda as I honor the great and caring person you were to me! Thank you for always believing in me as a writer! I look forward to reuniting with you in Heaven when it is time for God to call me home.

ACKNOWLEDGEMENTS

I am truly blessed to have such special people in my life, who I am so honored and grateful to have as my very special friends who care about me and love me and been a great support to me in my pursuit of writing this book. I want to acknowledge them and thank them for the gift they are to me, as they are my gifts from God.

My parents, Harley (Skeeter) and Vera Bowen – Thank you Mom and Dad for always loving me and believing in me and supporting my dreams and wishes.

My children, Shannon and Michael – Love you with all my heart!!

My grandchildren, Mckenzie and Colton – Love you two so very much!

Marsha Ledet – My wonderful friend who always believed so much in me!

Maradith Halvorson – Your friendship and kindness has always meant the world to me!

Diane Manthei – My sister in Christ, your caring and kind ways are so special to me!

Darren Gauck and Arden Schoep – You guys are the very best! Thank you for being so encouraging and supporting me in my decision to leave your employment so I could pursue my purpose and passion of writing this book. Loved working together as a team with you guys. I always felt like we were family. Thank you for the kindness and friendship you offered me. You always treated me like a Queen! You were gifts sent to me from God, and I am so truly honored to have gotten to spend years working with you.

These are only a few of the many wonderful people I have in my life. I am Blessed to have so many kind, loving and caring people that are very precious to me, and I thank you all for the gift of each and everyone of you! I am truly Blessed!

Chapter 1

LOVE AND INSPIRATION

I KNEW A TEACHER WHO would instill inspiration into his student's everyday by telling them, "you are the most precious gift on earth." Can you imagine how magnificent that would make those students feel? To have someone tell you continually that you are the most precious gift, would be so uplifting, and I would think it would just warm your heart every single day. How would you feel if someone said those words to you? Wouldn't it make you truly feel that you were capable of anything and everything? That there wasn't anything you couldn't do in this world. It would give you hope and inspire you for a great life! It would bring joy and happiness to you. It would make you smile and feel happy. Those students were so fortunate to have a teacher who could make that difference in their lives by stating those words to them. How wonderful it would be if each and every person on this earth could hear every day that they are the most precious gift on earth. What a difference that would make in our world today.

Those words are exactly how our God feels about us every day. We are the most precious gift to God, and HE loves us so very much. I wish people could see and feel how God feels about us. Sometimes in this cold and cruel world we become cynics as we see unjust happenings all around us. If we could just put aside the harshness circumstances in our world today and return to LOVE. Love is truly the answer for everything we do.

We need to think thoughts of love. So many things in life can turn us into bitter and angry people, but it is amazing how life changes when you can turn away from bitter and anger feelings and look at anyone who has hurt you, with love in your heart.

It is definitely not an easy thing to do, but in time and with prayer you can get to the point where you can see everyone through the eyes of only love, not hatred. Prayer is truly the answer to turn our lives away from hatred and to having love in our hearts for all.

We all have people in our lives who have hurt us tragically. We all have had bad things happen to us, as God never guaranteed us an easy life, but He did guarantee us

HIS LOVE always and that he would never leave us. He would always be at our side.

A few years ago when I was going through some difficult transitions in my life, and had experienced some health issues, I found myself feeling lost and empty, and desperately needing some direction in my life. I had gotten an email from an author, and she was talking about what God wanted from us in this life. I listened and read intently as I was really needing to know just what did God want from us in this life.

Chapter 2

RELATIONSHIP WITH GOD

S HE SAID GOD WANTS a one on one relationship with us, by us spending time talking to God every day, sharing our problems with HIM, really talking to God, sharing our lives with HIM. Making God a priority, by taking time in prayer and conversation with HIM daily on a consistent basis. Above all, taking the time to show gratitude and thankfulness for all the blessings he has bestowed on us in our lives, whether it was a large thing, like a new home or a small thing like having food in your refrigerator or a bed to sleep in, or the car you drive. To me, her words in having a relationship with God sounded so heavenly.

So that day my life was changed! I began spending an hour to an hour and a half with God every single day, depending on how much I need to discuss with my Lord, and still do that to this day, and how my life has changed for the better. Sometimes I have some spiritual booklets I may spend time reading out of during my prayer time with God, and sometimes I read scripture out of the Bible before or after my prayer time. I thank God for everything in my life, my family, my friends, my life, my church, my home but most of all I thank GOD for the gift that HE is in my life. I thank Him for the beautiful blue sky and the white puffy clouds, and for the gorgeous sunrise and sunsets. I pray for the homeless, the hungry, the needy and the sickly on a daily basis. I pray for good health for my family and friends. I thank God for the gift of life and letting me live each and every day. I thank God for the money in my bank account, so I can pay my bills and be able to have those resources to buy what I need to buy. Sometimes I just sit in quiet meditation to hear what comes to mind during those quiet sessions with God. It has changed my life. I truly feel like a different person, a person who is more caring, more compassionate, more kind, and by all means much more loving to everyone.

People I once felt dislike for I noticed I began to be able to pray for them, where I once felt anger towards them, and then my heart began to feel love and forgiveness for those people, and even began noticing how I had changed. I always felt these difficult people in my life needed to change, but really what it boiled down to was when my thoughts about them changed then it was amazing how those people then became a real blessing to me. It was so amazing to watch this with my very own eyes, to see the change in those relationships that once brought tears to my eyes as my heart was hurting so from the pain they had caused me in my life, and now I had tears of joy of how those relationships began to completely and totally turn around into loving and caring feelings.

The change in me was over the top. I even began to listen to my heart before speaking my opinion or judgment about something, and immediately thought of what would God or Jesus want me to do or say in this situation. I was able to "let go" of anything that bothered me or burdened me, just let it go to God, knowing in my heart that HE would take care of it, and that I didn't have to concern myself with that problem anymore.

Oh my, what a relief that was, no more worry or stress, just give it to God. Praise the Lord!!! Totally changed my life for the better!! It takes some time to be able to pray for people who have brought hurt into your life, but the more you pray and talk to God you find that your heart softens for everyone no matter what they ever did to you.

Time with God is the best gift you can give yourself because you begin to feel such peace in your heart, and time with God becomes a necessity in your life, like you can't go one day without having that quiet time with God. So hard for me to even imagine how to live on this earth without God guiding and directing my life and being there for me to turn to on an everyday level. I am so thankful for the time I have with God, because it brings calmness and serenity in my life. I feel that God is my best friend as I can talk to HIM about everything and about all that is on my mind and in my heart. When I have difficulties in life I can give my burdens to God and know in my heart all is well, as God will take care of it, and I can now let it go and not worry or stress over it because God has it handled. What peace that brings me!

I think of all the blessings God has given me in my lifetime. I remember when I was a young girl I would pray every night to God before I went to bed, always mentioning the things I wanted in life, and was always so happy that everything I asked for I always received, and I thought oh my what a wonderful God this is. All I have to do is ask and I receive, until one day when I was maybe 11 years old I did not receive the gift I wanted, and I was flabbergasted that God did not provide that for me. How dare

HE not give me my request. I was devastated, as I had so much hope and faith that God would give me anything I asked for, and when HE didn't I could not believe it. So I became mad at God and I quit praying to HIM. That was so foolish, but as a young child I believed whatever you ask God for HE will give it to you. I hadn't learned the whole truth of GOD, to recognize all HE has done in my life and the lives of all of us. How HE always watched out over me, always protected me and guided my life and kept me safe and well. That knowledge would come later in my life.

When I was about 16 years old I watched the movie Song of Bernadette, and that movie touched my life so deeply, and it even seemed to change who I was and who I became. I cried through the whole movie. I have seen the movie many times since. It was as though I now knew I'd be living a life by wanting God with me everyday, even though I did spend years away from God, that movie made me a kind and compassionate person or maybe those were gifts that God had put in me. I just know that movie really made a huge impact on me.

Spending time with God is the most important gift you can give yourself. God wants a one on one relationship with you. HE wants to hear about your life, about your day, about what troubles you and HE wants you to show your gratefulness to HIM by thanking HIM over and over for all of the many blessings HE has given you in your lifetime. Do you ever think about all the great things God has done for you? For a long time I never thought about it until I started to pray daily, and then I spent a lot of time thinking back on my life of all that had happened to me, good and bad, and all the lessons I had learned, and about how my life had turned out. How blessed I truly was, and never stopped to even consider that God had a hand in all of that until I started to pray daily.

Prayer opens your mind so much as you look at where you are in life and how you got there, and you didn't get there by yourself, as God was always by your side. What God wants is simple. HE just wants time with you, your undivided attention with quality time spent between the two of you. I am the example that it will change your life as it did mine. The more I prayed the more good things came into my life, and I would notice right away and think about what God was doing for me in my life, it was truly amazing!

What is keeping you from spending time with God? A time commitment issue? I know how we all are so very busy in our lives with all there is to do, as my life was that way too. I did make that commitment because I knew how much I needed God. I am an only child and when my parents passed away in 2001 and 2002 I was totally and utterly lost, not to mention devastated. I felt like an orphan, I was an orphan, as I had no siblings, my parents were gone, but fortunately I had my 2 grown children and 2 grandchildren that were my family. But something happened to me when I lost my parents. I lost myself.

When you are an only child you really have a close connection to your parents, because they are all you have before you have children of your own, and you are all they have, so they adore you and cherish you, at least mine did. My Dad was my best friend in the whole world. He was my confidant, my knight in shining armor, someone that was always there for me and loved me unconditionally. I could do no wrong in his eyes. I sought out advice from my Dad as he was such a wise man. Everything I accomplished in life I did it for him, to make him so proud of me. I wanted him to see how smart I was, and that I could do anything, and I loved being all I could be, not so much for me, but for him. He always loved and supported and encouraged me my whole life. Always taught me there wasn't anything I couldn't do in this life. He always had more faith in me than I had in myself. So it was an honor for me to do good and make him proud, as I felt I was the person I was because of him and the faith he had in me and all the encouragement he always gave me.

When my Dad died, I almost died too, because I didn't know how to live without him, because he was my reason for living and for having a good job with good pay, as I did it all for him to show him how good I had turned out thanks to all his support. So I lost my will to live, to go on, I cried everyday as I missed him terribly and wasn't prepared for his passing as we had no warning that this was going to happen. How could I live without

Dad? The wonderful father who loved me unconditionally. I missed his love so much. I was everything to him and he was everything to me. I was his little girl, no matter how old I was. At first I was so mad at God for taking my Dad from me, so I lived in anger for a long time. I barely was existing in this life, as I just was going through the motions of living, never smiling, never having joy, never laughing, but lived with sadness every day. I finally went into counseling to get the help I needed, and was in counseling for 2 years, but it did help me so much. I knew I had to go on with my life, as I know that is what Dad would want for me, and I had my children to live for, and my son lived with me and depended on me, so I had to be there for him and that is how I kept going by living for my children because they needed their Mom in their life.

It took years to get to the point of where I felt I could move on with my life, as the loss of Dad was just so overwhelming. I would visit my parents graves every week and sit there by their gravestones talking to them just like I did every single Sunday when I would visit them at their home when they were alive. I didn't know how to stop talking to them like I had done for years and years. Our time together was so special, so many wonderful moments we had. One day as I was in my car and driving to my parents graves my Mom appeared to me telepathically and said to me, "live your life," and she repeated it several more times. It all happened so fast. My first reaction was how could I be hearing from my

Mom since she is not alive on this earth any longer. It did freak me out at first, and certainly grabbed my attention. I was in shock as I listened to those words, and in my mind I could see my Mom's face, and then after hearing those words about 3 times she was gone. For the longest time I kept thinking what did she mean by that, as I was living my life or so I thought, but then I realized maybe she was just sending me this message to let me know she arrived safely in heaven. Maybe I wasn't living my life then being so consumed with grief and loss, and spending as much time as I could at their graves. I never thought for one moment I wasn't living my life, but am sure my Mom was saying that I didn't need to visit them so much because they weren't there, they were in the glory of heaven, and she was wanting me to know its okay to move on from my grief and begin a life for myself without them.

I came across this book about Heaven, and I feel like it really saved my life because it talked of how beautiful Heaven is and described the magnificence and amazement of heaven, and it gave me peace to know that my Dad and Mom were there in the paradise of heaven, and all of a sudden it was okay that they were there because I knew they were safe because they were in this glorious place of paradise that I read about in this book, so then I finally got the peace I needed. It was the acceptance that I longed for, knowing my parents were okay, and knowing they were free of their aging and ailing bodies, and that they were surrounded by joy and happiness. I then knew I could start living again because I knew that someday I would see them again and we could be together when it was my time to go to Heaven. So I then began to live my life, but it sure took me a long time to get there.

That's why I know God is what we need in our lives. God saved me from my anguish I was experiencing. HE came to my rescue and brought me peace and serenity once I began to turn to God in prayer. So I say to you please do this for you! It will change your life. God is waiting to hear from you, as HE wants a relationship with you. HE loves you with all of his heart, loves you unconditionally and wants to help you in your life and wants to be your friend!

Are you dealing with struggles in your life in relationships or financial, or maybe you have a job that you just can't stand and would like to live a life of being able to follow your dreams and what you are passionate about? If so, then I say to you, turn your eyes to GOD, and spend time everyday in prayer with HIM, talking to HIM, reading the Bible, reading inspirational books, but most important is to take the time to have one on one time with God. It will change your life in an abundant way. HE is waiting to hear from you, so don't hesitate.

We all have God given gifts and talents in each one of us. Sometimes it takes awhile to know what they are, but once you realize what gift God gave you, its so important to use that gift in this life. We come here to earth to fulfill our purpose and once we do fulfill our purpose, and follow our heart and our dreams, that is when we truly come alive. I believe our lives finally really make sense once we can see what it is we are to do. At least it did for me. Writing is my love and my passion and my dream.

My wish is to give hope and inspiration to as many people as I can. I want to make a difference in the lives of others. I want to be the difference. I want everyone to know just how your life can be so precious to you if you just begin by having a relationship with God. It's the single most important thing you can do for yourself. I know this from experience. For years I was drifting through life, and my life was all about survival, being able to pay the rent and utilities and buy food, always hoping for a better life for myself, for a better tomorrow. My struggles continued for years. But once I read in an inspirational book about what God truly wanted from us was a relationship, a one on one relationship with HIM, then I knew that is what I must do, I knew it in my heart. Time with God, to talk about our troubles and our burdens and give those burdens to God, a time to thank HIM for all the blessings HE has bestowed in our lives, a time to pray for others who are in need. My life changed dramatically when I began this process of daily time with God, and so can yours. You can finally have peace and joy in your life again, because God will grant that to you. HE just wants to hear from you, it is really very simple. The rewards you will receive by spending time with God is truly the most amazing experience you will ever have. I want the very best for you!

I want you to have what I've been given by spending time with God. Your heart softens, you find that love towards everyone is the answer to your life, and forgiveness is essential.

God will put peace in your heart, and love in your soul, and will give you so much joy!

Chapter 3

CHILDREN OF GOD

W E ARE CHILDREN OF God! What an amazing statement that is to be a precious child of God.

Just hearing those words makes us realize how blessed we truly are, that God loves us, protects us, and cares for us. The answer to all our problems in life is time with God in prayer and meditation!

Jeremiah 29:11: "For I know the plans I have for you," says the Lord. "They are plans For good and not for disaster, to give you a future and a hope."

Matthew 11: 28-29: Come to me, all you who are weary and burdened and I will give You rest. Take my yoke upon you and learn from me, for I am gentle and humble in Heart, and you will find rest for your souls.

Those are 2 great Bible verses that I feel really talk to us, as it shows that God is always there for us working on our behalf, protecting and guiding us, wanting the best for us.

However I feel we have to talk to God and pray to God, and begin a relationship with HIM, as we can't just sit idly waiting for a miracle. We need to reach out to God, ask for what we need. Give GOD our time and attention in thought and word and thankfulness.

Did you know your thoughts really become you? For example, if you think negatively, then negative things will come in your life, but if you turn it around and only think positive thoughts then good things will come into your life. It is so true! It is so easy to think negatively, and it takes real effort to turn it around and think positive thoughts, but it is something that will really change your life. Change your thoughts, change your life!

Begin today! Change your life with positive thoughts. Begin to pray everyday, it doesn't have to be an hour or hour and a half like I do. It can be 15 minutes, which can turn out to be the best 15 minutes of your life everyday. I'd like to believe we all have 15 minutes to give to GOD to show our thankfulness, and to bring peace into your hearts, and love into your souls. I hope you will give yourself that gift! It will make all the difference in the world in the quality and well being of your life.

Years ago I found this little Morning Prayer that I thought was just a perfect way to start my day. It goes like this:

I get up in the morning, to face another day, and wonder what's in store for me along Life's traveled way. Before I start to do my work with all its toil and care, I stop and lift

My eyes to God and offer up a prayer. I thank HIM for the life I have, the strength to do my work. I ask him to assist me with the things I shouldn't shirk. I also pray for others, The sick, the lame, the blind, for those who work with people a better life to find.

This little talk I have with God just starts my day off right. The things I do seem easier from morning until night. So first thing in the morning do this without delay; ask God for

Strength and guidance, you'll have a better day.

Isn't that a nice prayer to start your day?

There are always going to be people we may know who are challenging and difficult.

The key is to know how to have relationships with people who are unlike us. That has always been a struggle for many of us. Who doesn't like to avoid those people if we can, but sometimes they end up being people we have to have a relationship with, as they could be a co-worker, a parent, a child, a boss, a sister, a brother, an in-law, etc.

We have to find a way to tolerate them and to somehow make peace with them. For myself I have had some wonderful bosses, and I have had a few horrible bosses as well, and maybe that is the case for you too. For years, if I found myself in a situation like that

I would leave that job, because I don't like conflict and I knew I was not going to subject myself to that any longer, so I did the only thing I knew how to do and that was escape.

That is, until I began to have a wonderful relationship with God, and I came to believe that we have to pray for those challenging people in our lives, and we also need to look at them as children of God and that there is much good in them, even if we can't see it at the time. The most difficult people in the world are the ones dealing with much pain in their own lives, and need our understanding more than ever. I began to pray for the people in my life that I had problems with, and you wouldn't believe the change in them that occurred. They became the most joyful people to be around. I actually could not believe what was happening with them. I began to look at them through the eyes of love in my prayer time. It was the hardest thing ever to pray for people who brought unhappiness and sorrow to my life, but once you can do that you can see the changes that start to take place within them. It is amazing, it truly is! Those challenging relationships began to be joyous relationships all because I prayed for them and God makes it happen!

There are so many people in the world that are unhappy in their jobs, and I know what that is like because in my career I have experienced that from time to time. One day I decided to look at my job as a blessing, more than a curse. I started feeling appreciative of the blessing of my paycheck, my health insurance and all my benefits. I also began to think of how I was a blessing to the company I worked for and all that I provided at my job. I became so thankful that I had a job with a nice paycheck and a car that got me to that job. So when you become distraught over the job that you dislike just take a few moments to think of how you are a blessing to that job, to the company, to the people and all of your surroundings there. Again its positive thinking, instead of negative thinking. It will change your life!

What improvements would you like to see in your life? Do you have a Mother-in-law you cannot tolerate, or are you having problems with your child, or do you wish for a better paying job, or maybe a whole new career? We all have issues that we would like to see improved. All our problems and our burdens is what God is waiting for you to give to HIM in prayer, so HE can help you, so HE can give you Peace in your heart, and so HE can be your Savior. GOD desperately wants to help all of HIS children, HE is just waiting to hear from you. Once you give your burdens to GOD you can rest in knowing it is now in God's hands, HE will take care of it. You just have to keep praying!

Giving in service to others is what God wants of us, and we do receive so much more in return than what we give to others. Helping others, doing good deeds, being of service is what we are called to do. I remember when I worked for a Catholic Church as a Bookkeeper and Administrative Assistant, I also became a Food Pantry Director and

Director of a church fund that assisted low income families. Holding those two Director titles gave so much back to me in rewards. The families I fed through the food pantry was such a great feeling to be able to help them, as I just felt so much joy in my heart as I could see the faces light up of these people who were so happy to get food, and was especially moved to see the childrens faces become so joyful when they saw the food they were getting. I felt truly inspired by being able to help these families. I would go home at night feeling so proud of the contributions I made each day of helping others.

It was the same for me when I assisted families who were about to be evicted because they couldn't pay their rent due to loss of a job, and the families who were going to have their utilities shut off as they didn't have the money to pay for them. I worked with many landlords and utility companies pleading with them to not evict families or turn off utilities as I explained we at the church would see the money was given to them. I would have fundraisers to raise those funds needed to help the low income, and loved being able to help those families in need. It brought such joy into my life knowing the good deeds I was doing for those people. I received much support from the church as they helped me put these fundraisers together to feed the hungry and assist the poor. Those were wonderful days for me when I was helping others on a daily basis.

I love the verse of, *"This is the Day the Lord has made, Let us Rejoice and Be Glad In It"*.

What does that bring to mind for you when you say those words? Everyday when I have my prayer time and I say that verse I immediately think of the blessings of that day, as I think about my day and feel joy of what that day brought for me, and I silently recite the goodness of that day, as I paused to reflect on the day and all that it brought to me. Even if it wasn't the brightest day of your life, you can still always find a Blessing in the day, even if it was just the sunshine or the beautiful blue sky or the gorgeous sunset.

Another verse I recite at prayer time is *"Trust In The Lord With All Your Heart, Lean*

Not On Your Own Understanding, But Acknowledge HIM In All Ways and Know HE

Will Guide Your Path." That verse always brings joy to me, knowing in my heart that I can always and forever trust the Lord with all my heart, and know HE will always take care of things and protect me and guide my life. What a peaceful feeling that is!

Another thing I say to God in my daily prayer time is, *"I love you With All My Heart,*

All My Soul and All my Might." I say that a number of times in my prayer time.

That is how I feel for Jesus and God and the Angels, as I know they are there for each one of us everyday. Trust in Faith not my Sight. Know in your heart that they are always there for you, waiting to hear from you, waiting to hear that communication from us, that one on one time for us to delight in our Lord by giving our time and attention to the Almighty.

Did you know that God has a perfect plan for your life? A plan for us far greater than we could ever imagine ourselves. God never gives us everything all at once, but just step by step, HE truly wants to teach us to "walk by faith", not by sight. God will Bless your life so much if you just put HIM first in your life, and spend time with HIM daily, talking to him, sharing your thoughts and feelings and your burdens, and the things that bring anxiety and worry into your life. God seeks to help you, as HE wants you to share your life with HIM. It will bring you many rewards in your life if you will do this.

One of my favorite prayers is the Serenity Prayer. If you are not familiar with it, it goes like this:

"God grant me the serenity to accept the things I cannot change, the courage to change the things I can, and the wisdom to know the difference." This is a remarkable prayer. It has guided me throughout my life. There are things we do have to accept even if it is difficult to do so, but this prayer reminds us that we just have to ask God to grant *u*s the peace to accept those challenges in our lives that we cannot change.

However, we can ask God for the courage to change the things we can, what we do have control over, and that can be our thoughts, our attitudes, our words, and our actions. All of those we do have control over, so that is what we can change in our lives. The best part of this prayer is the word 'wisdom", the wisdom to know the difference. We really do become wise once we stop and think and focus and realize what we can change in our lives and what we can't. That is when wisdom comes to us and teaches us the difference.

Another prayer that has much meaning to me is the Prayer of Protection. This prayer has had such an impact on my life, and I know it could be that way for you too as you contemplate the words and let it really sink into your being as you recite them. It goes like this:

The Light of God Surrounds Us,
The Love of God enfolds us;
The Power of God protects us,
The Presence of God watches over us;
Wherever we are God IS!

I just adore this prayer and love to recite it and really feel in your heart what each word is representing in your life. Just knowing and believing that God does indeed surround you, enfold you in HIS Love for you. God protects you and watches over you at all times, and wherever you are God IS! Just feel the meaning of those words. Knowing in your heart how important and valuable you are to God. We are all HIS children, and HE adores us all! Loves each and everyone of us unconditionally.

A great Bible verse that I feel really speaks to us is: *"My Love for you will never end Says the Lord."* Isn't that just the most precious words you have heard? God says HIS

Love for us will never end, so that is forever and ever. We are HIS most precious gift! His Love will always be with us. It will never ever end, its forever, its eternity! Amazing!

Trust in God at all times. Pour out your heart before HIM. God is a refuge for us!

Jesus is with us Always. HE continues this promise to us all who is listening. You, who listen and acknowledge will be Blessed beyond measure! Look at Jesus through the eyes of your heart.

I have to share this story with you about my life and how it has evolved over the last few years. 5 years ago I was living in a mobile home, and then God Blessed me by opening up that door of opportunity that took me to a lovely home to rent where I lived for several years. Then God once again opened another opportunity for me by helping me find a larger home, and one that was the most beautiful, a home that I never ever even imagined I would have the Blessing of living in. It was all GOD! He did this for me! I think of this so many times of all the ways God has Blessed my life. I never could have done any of this by myself. HE guides and directs my journey in this life. All HE asks of us is to acknowledge HIM, to pray, to spend time with, to thank HIM for the many

Blessings and Gifts HE has given to you and to all of us. Many rewards will be given to you when you come to know and believe and have faith and trust in GOD, and to spend time in your lives reflecting on all you have been Blessed with. All God wants is time with you, quality one on one time where you open your heart and talk and share to God about your life and about your desires. HE just wants a relationship with us! Can you give Him that? If you do, you will be justly rewarded emotionally, physically and spiritually.

God Loves YOU! He wants the very best for you. He wants to bring you joy and Happiness! We were never promised a life on this earth without pain and suffering. But we were promised a life where God would never forsake us, never leave us, but always be with us every single moment of our lives. He lives in your heart, in your soul, and in your mind if you will just let HIM in. He will bring good things into your life. HIS plan for your life is the best, better than you could ever imagine. However, we have to know that what we want in our lives comes in God's timing, not ours, so we have to be patient and have faith and trust and know that God will help you when you call out to him.

Chapter 4

GIVE OUR WORRIES
TO GOD

H AVE PATIENCE BUT TALK to God, share your life, your worries, your concerns, your dilemmas in life, your wants and needs but never forget to thank HIM for the many blessings HE has given you everyday of your life. Thank Him for everything!

God has a great plan for your life, more than you could ever imagine. HE plans for good and wonderful things to come to you that will fulfill you with hope and a future. We just have to keep believing all positive and great things are coming into your life and keep praying, and believing all good is coming to you, greater good than what you could think of for yourself. God has that master plan for each of our lives, and it is so important we believe it in our hearts.

We who are burdened with the many worries and concerns we have on our minds, all we have to do is give those burdens to God, and HE will give you rest. He will take care of our burdens and worries and concerns, so we can rest peacefully knowing its now in

God's hands and HE will take care of it and you no longer have to concern yourself with it. You can now rest and have peace in your heart!

Psalm 23:6 Surely goodness and love will follow me all the days of my life, and I will Dwell in the house of the Lord forever.

Another great scripture. Goodness and love will follow you if you just let Jesus and God into your hearts and into your lives through prayer and praise to God.

Time with God is the best and most peaceful time of your life. I personally look forward each and everyday of my time with God. It sooths my soul, uplifts my spirit and gives me endless peace and serenity in my life. It is your time to talk to God to share what is going on in your life. HE really wants to hear from you. HE wants to know what concerns you have and what the desires of your heart are. He wants that one on one time with his child, YOU! He loves you so much, as you are His precious child who He is totally devoted to.

No one will ever love you like Jesus and God do! You will be truly amazed by the changes in your life, emotionally and physically, when you take the time for God.

Always be thankful for all the blessings God has brought into your life! Praise and honor God for his mercy, kindness, and compassion

HE shows to us all! Thank HIM for your family, friends, your home, your life, and truly look at your life and see all the many blessings God has given you throughout your whole life. Even thank God for the bed you sleep in that gives you rest. Thank him for your car that gets you where you need to go, and for the food that is in your refrigerator, that nourishes your body. Thank Him for your health, the most important gift we could receive. The list goes on and on of all the things in our lives we can thank God for, because we have been given so much!

To connect with God is when your life changes for the better. You may be going through your life without spending time with God and think your life is going okay, or you may feel God has abandoned you with so much going wrong in your life. God never abandons us, but sometimes we abandon God. We give up on hope and live in that place of sadness and regrets, and we allow ourselves to think only negative thoughts. It is vital we turn to GOD during those low times in our lives, as HE is the only answer for us.

He will in turn uplift and inspire you, give you hope and spending time with God really brings you back to love as you feel the love and peace of God in your heart. I'm telling you all of this through experience and knowledge, as this is how I found myself, my true calling, but most of all its where I found love and compassion for all. My whole being became new and different as I felt love and hope and inspiration and peace, all from spending time with God. Pouring out my heart to him, shedding many tears, healing my wounds, becoming emotionally and physically healed in my heart and soul. I cannot put into words the greatness of how I felt once I began spending time with God. I truly became a new person. I was always caring and loving, but now I'm more appreciative for all I have and all I am. I'm more positive and love myself and my life. I love others more than I ever did before, and some who I didn't see with loving eyes I now do see them through the loving eyes of God. We all are children of God. We all have good in us, and the people who are the most difficult need our love and understanding more than anyone else. You learn all of these things through spending time with God, as you become more Christ like yourself. Such a transformation your life becomes.

I love the phrase, **"change your thoughts, change your life"**. My life was changed because of the change in my thoughts. Begin to make that transformation of changing your thoughts to positive thinking, and you will see the changes in your life too.

Chapter 5

GIVING TO OTHERS

E ACH AND EVERY ONE of us has been blessed with God given
gifts. It is so vital that we use the gifts that have been given to us.
These are precious gifts from God to use in making our world a better
place and for the betterment of the people in our world. Your gift may
be providing help and assistance to others. It always seems we receive so
many rewards back when we reach out to others in service. In my life, as
a Food Pantry Director and Director of a fund that assisted low income
and needy people, I recall the many rewards given back to me in numerous
ways. I would have people thank me over and over again for the assistance
I provided for them. Many would hug me in appreciation, some would
send me thank you cards and some would call me their angel sent from
God above. All of their gratitude meant the world to me. It melted my
heart, and made me feel so good inside for the gift I could be to them
and their families. There was no better feeling for me than feeding the
hungry and providing assistance to the low income. I also worked as an
employment training assistant where I was given the blessing of finding
training jobs for the elderly. So many of them just wanted to still feel

productive in their lives by being able to still learn new skills in the job force and providing a service to a company and earning a paycheck. So many had felt that there was no hope in employment for them and what a difference it made in their lives knowing they could still be useful in the work world. It raised their self esteem and their confidence as this journey began for them. Once again they were so thankful for how I had helped them. Rewards for helping others is the best! So what gift did God give you? What area of your life seems to be calling your name? Maybe you would love to be a painter or possibly might want to work with young children. Or maybe working with animals is what you love the most.

The best way to find what moves you, or where your purpose or passion is, is if you stop and think about what would you do in a job for free. If you were given the opportunity to do something in life as a career and you could choose anything you wanted, what would that be? I've always felt writing was my calling, and would be happy to write with no pay because I love it. So that may be a question you ask yourself. What would you do without receiving a paycheck for? I believe that is how you find the gift of your life. We have heard people say, "follow your dreams." Easier said than done, huh? But yet I do think we find our true selves when we can follow our dreams, our passion. What moves you? What interests do you have? Is it politics or is there something that you feel really strongly about and wish things were different? That could be the sign that you could step up and make that difference by getting involved in whatever area in the world where you would like to see change. Be the change you wish to see in the world! Find your niche in our world, and there you will find your heart, your passion and your calling.

How many people do you know who work at jobs they cannot stand, but do it only for that almighty paycheck? How valuable are their lives? To work at a job you detest would be the worst thing ever. Just think about how that could affect your health and your stress level. To spend 40 hours every week drudgingly going to a job where they have no happiness. Why not seek out where you fit in the world in a career that makes your heart smile, and brings joy into your life? Just think of the difference of what your life would be like if you could be joy filled in your workplace. The difference in that person would be astounding, and amazing. Their outlook on life would be different. I bet they would be more positive about their lives. So if you are a person who feels agony about your job then I plead with you to please look at your life, and make the change you need to have a happier, more fulfilled life in your career path. It's so important to live our lives in a happy state, as this is the only life we have, and we have to live in the present moment as that is all that is promised, this very moment. Life, as we know, is too short to live in regret, pain or suffering because of choices we may have made. The time is now to choose joy, to choose happiness. My Mother once said to me, "live your life" and of course, at the time, I thought I was living my life, but much later I knew she was trying to tell me to quit grieving over my loss, and to move on with my life and begin to live again. If we could see or hear God I know HE would tell us to live for now, live in the moment, because tomorrow is never promised to us. Of course, we like to think of our futures and our goals that we may have, but it is important not to forget about living for now also!

Chapter 6

LOSS AND GRIEF

THEY SAY BY THE time we become 50 years old we have had to go through the experience of losing a loved one, either as a family member or a friend. The loss of important people in our lives is devastating, and so hard to work through. 8 years ago I lost my very best friend. Her name was Linda, and we had been friends for 33 years, and never did I ever think she would die and leave me long before our time. She was like a sister to me. We were opposite in so many ways, but yet alike in ways too, and we thought the same about almost everything. We could finish each other's sentences. I knew her so well and she knew me. We loved each other and loved spending time together.

She passed away at only 58 years old. She was planning a trip to France for the two of us, with her family inheritance she would be getting soon. Her heritage was French and she longed to go to France, so we were looking forward to our trip, but we never got to go because of her untimely passing from this earth. Linda was an exceptional person and I was so proud to call her my best friend. We always talked about growing old together and enjoying life as elderly people, and I was sure we would get to do that. But God called her HOME, and so I had to accept that, and I knew she had finally found happiness in her Heavenly Home. I gave the eulogy at Linda's funeral. Such a difficult thing to do, but yet I wanted to make sure that everyone knew at the funeral what a gift she was to me and to anyone who knew her. She was a nurse, and cared so much about people. Some of her ashes were given to me, in a special urn that reads "my best friend Linda" on the outside of the small urn. Grief is a very difficult transition to experience and to go through, but yet it is vital that we work through the grieving process in order to heal. It doesn't mean that we will ever stop missing the person who dies, but the process of grieving helps us move on in our lives. To grieve seems to soften our hearts as we continue to think of the person who meant so much to us. At times we wonder how will we live without them, but we do find a way to go on, as we must. I always find comfort knowing I will get to be reunited with my family members and friends who have passed from this world, and what a great reunion that will be. Linda was my biggest supporter in my writing. She thought I was a great writer and when I entered my first writing contest and was one of the winners she gave me a statue of a deer and an angel because that first story was about a deer and a family in the forest, and she knew I loved angels so she presented that gift to me representing her faith in me as a writer, and I still have it today.

She always encouraged me to write, but for many years I didn't, because I got caught up in being busy earning a living as a single mom and supporting me and my son, and that was my focus for many years. So I dedicate this book to my friend Linda.

Our friends in life can truly be our angels, as they are unbelievably amazing gifts to us from God. Our friends support and encourage us in our life journey, and are so special and so uplifting, and believe in our gifts and talents so very much. They can be our cheerleaders on earth. God sends us special people to be our friends on this earth, and they truly are gifts sent by God! I have great and wonderful Christian friends who are like my sisters. I would be lost without them, as they make such a difference in my life. I don't believe there are any coincidences in life, and I believe God sends to us in life the exact people that we need. I am so grateful to HIM for providing this network of friends who have made such an impact on my life. I am sure that is true for you too. I am sure great friends have come into your life as well. They are sent to us to influence and encourage us. If your friends are not doing that for you, I encourage you to find friends that will do that for you. I thank God everyday for my friends who are a true blessing!

I hope I'm a gift to them as well. I love to uplift and inspire people, and to be encouraging, to make a difference in their lives, to be that blessing or offer that glimmer of hope to those who need it. I love talking to people about Jesus and God, as I know HE is the answer to our lives. It is strange how sometimes it takes many years to really be able to see clearly the gift God is to us. For me, I always loved God, and would offer a small prayer every night before going to sleep, and sometimes talk to God during the day for a moment or two. But once I truly felt that God wanted more of me, more time with me, did I really understand the full impact of how my life would be. Once I began my daily time in prayer and conversation with God, I then could feel in my heart how desperately I needed God to this degree. How had I not known this before now? It is because I never took the time to find out. We know what our lives are like, and how full and busy we become, where we are dashing here or there, and having many tasks to do and much responsibilities in our lives, and sometimes barely have time to breathe, let alone think of taking the time to pray. But once I took the time to listen to my intuition and my heart telling me this is what I need to do, I finally paid full attention to inner nudging and began my journey with my Lord. It was so indescribably magnificent that I knew I had to share my knowledge and understanding of this amazing experience. What

I really wished was that it would not have taken me so many years to learn this. I felt like my life could have been so much more improved had I learned the magnitude of this Blessing much earlier in my life. I thought of how I might not have had so many difficult years had I known this long ago. But you can't look back in the past, you must look into the present moment and how it can affect your future by being given this gift of knowledge NOW. So I am here to give you this knowledge of the true blessings you will have in your lives if you give your time in prayer to God and Jesus. It totally changed my life 100% for the better. My heart became so open to receiving and giving love unconditionally, and only seeing everyone through the eyes of love.

My heart softened, and I never felt so much peace and joy in my life as I now did when I began to spend time everyday with God. This is what God wants of us.

He really wants a relationship with us. He wants us to talk to HIM about our wants and our desires, and for us to tell HIM what worries or concerns we have. HE wants only joy and happiness for us, and HE will help us have that, if we only will commit by taking the time with God on a regular basis. He so wants to know HIS children on a one on one basis. HE wants to hear from us every day. He wants us to keep HIM close to us, and turn to HIM for all things.

Chapter 7

TIME WITH GOD

W E ARE CHILDREN OF God! What an amazing statement! It sends chills down my spine, just by thinking of how we are all children of God, and how truly Blessed we are! We are loved unconditionally by our God!! Isn't that just the most wonderful feeling and thought? Loved unconditionally!

How many minutes a day do you give to God? I have learned that with every decision I need to make that I take time to turn to God and ask God to help me make the decision, as I trust Him with all my heart, to show me the right answer. How many times have you had such a time in making a decision on something important in your life? You may keep going back and forth with the answer, and it can be so frustrating not knowing what you should exactly do. That is when the answer is to take time to turn it over to

God or to ask God, what shall I do? The answer will come in your heart and you will know. It is amazing how that works. For me, I spend my quality time with God in increments of one hour a day, sometimes an hour and a half, depending on all I need to discuss with God. It is the best part of my day, as I feel so much love from God as

I spend that time with HIM. But you may not have an hour or more to devote to prayer, maybe it would be best for you to break it up through the day to spend time with

God, but what I believe is the most important in spending time with God, is to go to that quiet, private room, wherever that may be. It could even be outside in nature.

Sometimes I feel so connected to God when I'm outside with the birds, flowers and trees surrounding me. So it is wherever you feel most connected to God's presence. I do encourage you to find the time to spend with God. There is nothing like it in the world!

I believe it heals you on the inside, it gives you peace, comfort and joy. Answers can come to you as far as helping you make decisions in life, and the healing of your heart begins. I am speaking from experience, as I was forever changed inside and out. The outpouring of love I began to feel for everyone was totally amazing. It was as though

I was just consumed with never ending love for everyone, and I felt God's love for me so very strong too. My life began to change for the better. Wonderful things began to show up in my everyday life. I believe so much of what was happening to me, was the change in me, as I was always thinking so positively, and not allowing negativity into my conscious, because God was instilling so much love in me through our quiet times together. I began to feel more joyous everyday once I began to spend time with God, and again, I believe it was the love I was feeling from God, the love HE was putting in my heart, from our one on one time together.

I never felt so good about life and living in this life as I did when I began to spend quality time with God. I began to be more appreciative of everything I had been given. Each day became such a gift to me. I began thanking God for all the blessings and gifts HE has given me and was so grateful. I really started appreciating all that I had in my world.

Some things I never even thought about thanking God for, such as the air I breathe, the sight I see, the sounds I hear, to be able to walk and talk and for the gift of each new day.

It is all the little things in life that we never take time to notice the value of each one.

Until I began my time with God I never even thought about the regular things in life that I have but never showed appreciation for. So it is all so enlightening when you spend time with God. You finally see all the gifts and the blessings that surround you, that we easily can take for granted each and everyday. It felt so great to be able to show my appreciation and my gratitude for all the little things and the big things too, like my home, my job, the gift of the people in my life. These are all things I never thought of thanking God for and was so glad I could now show my appreciation in giving thanks and praise to God.

Life is so short, so be sure to have no regrets, and forgive those you need to forgive and let it go, and enjoy each and every day as a gift given to you from God. It is so important to live each day to the fullest, and to live in the moment of NOW, and this DAY because as I have said previously, tomorrow is never promised to us.

I always say why worry or feel anxious when you can pray and give your burdens to God. That is what God wants from us, to share our concerns with HIM, and watch and see how HE provides the answers and support for us. Calmness really does come when you talk to God about your fears and anxieties.

My daughter was diagnosed with a hernia, and it took so very long for her to recover. I remember clearly how she suffered after the surgery, and I can still see the grimacing look on her face as she tried standing and walking. Nothing hurts so much as to see your child in pain, it just totally is heart wrenching as you sit idly by knowing there is nothing you can do but to be there for her with comfort. It was months before she fully recovered, and lived on pain medication for a very long time, and how rejoicing it was when the day finally came months later when she could live pain free with no pain medication. I can still feel the relief in my heart as I heard this news.

So the following year when my daughter told me that she had to have another hernia surgery, I was totally devastated.

Thoughts whirled around in my head as I began to remember all she suffered before and all she went through for a very long time. I couldn't bear the thought of watching her live through this once again. I was consumed with worry, so I began to pray every single day wholeheartedly to God to ask HIM to please just make it leave my daughter's body, to just make it go away, as all things are possible with GOD. I would spend so much time in prayer and sobbing as my mind was consumed with memories of what she went through before, and how I could not see her go through this again. I prayed diligently for days and weeks, reaching out with all my might to our Almighty God and in my heart I believed that HE would heal her somehow, but I still continued to pray everyday without ceasing. Then one day the miracle came!! My daughter contacted me to tell me the good news!! She had gone to her doctor for an ultrasound of her hernia, and much to the amazement of everyone, there was NO

HERNIA inside her body!!!! Unbelievable! I gasped, and felt overjoyed with this fabulous news. What was now in her body was just a cyst, and it would be removed through a more simple procedure. HURRAY! A more simple surgery with a shorter recovery time, and a faster healing process, so much easier on her body, I was thankful.

No hernia!! Praise The Lord!!! I can't even describe my feelings at that time. I was so overcome with the gift that God gave me that day, in knowing my daughter did no longer have a hernia, as it had been removed and vanished from my daughter's body!

OMG, the miracle of it all, and God had granted my prayer, and saved my daughter from not having a hernia. I was overjoyed and thanked

God over and over again. I was over the moon with happiness and joy! My daughter's first hernia turned out to be very rare and she was in surgery for 4 hours because of the difficult position it was in, as they had to work around removal of it and not cut a main artery because if they had she could have bled to death. The thought of her having to go through that again with it being that serious and that dangerous of a surgery just scared me to death. So thank God the surgeon had a very steady hand, as I prayed so much before that surgery for it to be successful with no complications. So now, we have just learned that there is no longer a hernia in her body, just a cyst that would need to be removed, and a simple procedure.

It brought me to tears and more excitement than I can ever remember. However it did turn out to be removed surgically to make sure they got it all, but her recovery was so quick and it seemed like the healing began almost immediately, and she was feeling great again within a week and what a Blessing that was that she was bouncing back so quickly. Praise the Lord! Thank you God for healing my daughter so fast. So you see my dear readers, miracles do come true, if you believe with all your heart, and if you take the time to have a relationship with our God. God wants to help you every step of the way in this life. HE always is here for you. I'm the example of how this can happen!

The key is to spend time with God daily, always PRAISE HIM and always show your GRATITUDE daily to God for all that He has given you in this life, every single blessing that you have. God LOVES you with all His heart, and wants to provide the desires of your heart!

Another family incident that happened was a horrible crash on the interstate near where my daughter and her family lives. It involved a bus, a semi and many cars and a huge fire on the highway. As soon as I heard about it I called my daughter and asked where my grandchildren are, and she said on a bus going to a choir contest.

I absolutely froze when she said that!! My daughter was sure that the bus had gone much earlier, long before this Interstate crash. It turned out that some of the kids were late getting on the bus for that choir contest so their bus was delayed in getting started.

However they ended up on the interstate right after the crash, and were delayed for hours on the interstate while it was being cleaned up from the fire and the injured people. So once again, I believe in my heart, it was ALL GOD protecting my grandchildren from danger and from possibly being severely hurt from that accident. I pray everyday for the safety and well being for my children and grandchildren, as I always ask God to keep them safe from all harm, and free from all illness and disease. It was no accident that some of the kids arrived late to get on their bus, and no accident that the bus they were on got that late start that day. It was all part of God's plan to keep my grandchildren and the other children safe from harm. Again, another miracle from God! He hears our prayers, our concerns, and is here to help us in our time of need and to protect our families when we spend time in prayer.

When we give God our time, and build a relationship with God, as HE always longs to hear from us, I believe He will be there for us protecting us and our families. I know with all my heart that God caused the delay that day for my grandchildren so they would be kept from harm. I thank God everyday for all that He does in my life, and for keeping my family safe and well and protected. Isn't it worth it for you to keep your families safe?

God is waiting to hear from you, always waiting for us to acknowledge HIM in our lives for all that He does for us. It's never too late to begin a relationship with God!

I attended my granddaughter's high school graduation, and they had such wonderful speakers in attendance, and I was immediately struck by one teacher's comments about "The Dash". Have you heard about the Dash? It is an email that I've seen for several years that seems to get passed around to many peoples emails, and it is very meaningful. This teacher explained it so exquisitely. The Dash is what we do in our lives once we go out into the world. It is how we live our lives. The teacher was encouraging all of the students to go out into the world to make a difference, to uplift and inspire others, and to be the difference in the world. No matter what field of study each graduate chooses, that wherever life takes them, to take the time to give hope and inspiration to others in life, and to be that blessing to others and to make a difference.

His speech was truly uplifting, and his words were so perfect, as he was filled with enthusiasm for all that each student could be to others, and how they could truly make a difference in the world. One of the best speeches I have ever heard, and we all were touched by his words and his gift of speaking, and the gift he was to each one of those students at that high school.

I have been told by people that say to me "you are such a light." It's such a great compliment and I never quite know how to respond when I am told that, because it always takes me by surprise. In thinking about it though, it is not me that is the light, it is the Christ light that shines from within me, and it glows and beams to the outward of my being. My Christ light shines from the inside out. It makes me so happy that I have that light within myself, and that the light of Jesus lives inside of me and reflects and glows on the outside of my body. Oh, how I love my God with all my heart, all my soul, all my might and all my strength as HE is my rock and my salvation, and I have a continual relationship with my God! How about you? Would you like to have the "light that shines from you" too? You can, it is all up to you. God is waiting! HE wants to hear from you. He wants a relationship with you.

All it takes is to spend time talking to God, sharing your burdens with Him, praying to God, thanking God, praising God for the many blessings HE has bestowed on your life every single day! He SO wants to hear from you, His child, His child of God! I hope you will seek God, so you too can have Peace, Love and Comfort in your heart and also have the Christ light that shines out of you. Wouldn't you love to have all of that? Start today! Begin a new life for yourself, one that offers love to you, and peace and joy and comfort. God loves you for the person that you are!

I want you to have the great life I have in accepting God in your heart. HE is always there for you, inside you, beside you, holding your right hand and holding you as you are a treasure to HIM! It will change your life for the better, as it did mine!

I pray that you will accept God in your heart on this very day, as you are reading this.

Have you ever thought of the word "free", and really contemplated what that word means to you? Freedom can represent a lot of things in your life. It most definitely says freedom to be you, to be the lovely, unique, precious person you are.

Freedom can also mean "letting go." Many people who have wounds and scars and damage done to them need healing. They can release and let go of all the pain that still lives in their heart. You can just release it to God, and allow it to leave your body by giving it over to God, so that you know longer feel the pain that has held you back for so long. How delightful it can feel to release the wounds and the pain. Talk about being free! That process truly gives you the opportunity to open your heart to living again, as the pain is released from your heart and your soul. You wouldn't believe all the people that have a closed heart because of all they have suffered in their lives. They protect themselves by building a wall around their hearts so that no more pain can enter. The only way I know of releasing that pain is to let it go, and give it to God, and the peace you receive once you have done that is overwhelming, because now you are free to live with an open heart instead of a blocked and closed heart. Is this person you? Could you be someone who has never been able to let go of the pain? We can forgive people in our lives and believe in our hearts it is over and done with, as you have forgiven, but what I know is that until you have actually and totally let it go by giving it to God to be released, then it can still linger in your heart. So many things in life can cause long lasting pain. It could be the loss of a loved one, it could be abuse you may have suffered, or it could be a family member who has hurt you deeply. People I know that have lived with abuse are in need of letting that go, as hard as it is, as it is a necessity to live a happy and peaceful existence. Embrace the worthiness of your life by not allowing that abusive person to control your thoughts and your fears any longer. It is so freeing once you can really trust

God and letting it all go to God by releasing the wounds, the scars, the fears and the damage you have felt. You are now free to feel goodness, joy and love!

Chapter 8

DECEASED LOVED ONES

T HERE ARE MANY PEOPLE who have deceased loved ones that they still cannot get over the grief, even many years after the loved one has passed. I remember when my Dad passed away it took me 5 years to heal from the loss of him in my life, as he was my Rock and my best friend. He loved me so much and always believed in me and supported me and always thought that I could do anything I set my heart intention to do. I would strive to be the best I could be to make him proud of me! I loved my Dad so much, and when he left me I didn't know how to live without him, because he was my everything, and I lost myself for awhile but prayer and God got me through it all. I could not have gotten through it without my strong Faith and my Belief in God. Even though you never totally get over losing the special people in your life, you do learn how to go on and live your own life, and knowing in your heart that your loved one will always carry a special place inside of you, so the memory of the happy times with that person will always be with you.

But there are people who still suffer from so much sadness years and years after that person has passed. They don't seem to ever move on from the grief, and how very sad it is that people get stuck in their unhappiness and cannot get over their loss.

I feel deep empathy for those people, and pray you find a way to move on, as that is what your deceased love one would want for you. They would not want you unhappy. To those people in that situation, I say to you, let the sadness go, and rejoice in the fact that you were blessed to have that person in your life for as many years as you did.

Yes, that person has now descended into Heaven and you cannot see them anymore. I encourage you to be happy for them that they are free from the pain they may have suffered here on earth and that they are in the glorious land of Heaven with Jesus and

God and be happy for them. Too many people stay stuck in their own loss to be able to be happy for those who are now free of pain. Release your pain and let it go to God, so that you too can live again, and when you think of the loved one who has passed, remember the blessing and the gift that person was to you, and the happy times you had.

Your loved one would not want you spending your life in pain and unhappiness. They would want you to go on with your life, to be happy, and to live your own life. I pray for no more suffering for you, and that you too can release your sadness, your grief and your pain to God, by letting it go to God so you may live again. Rejoice in the fact that you will see your loved one again when God calls you HOME to

HEAVEN, and will have a glorious reunion with our pets and with our loved ones who are there waiting for us. I just can't even imagine how amazing Heaven will be, with our Jesus and our God, and all our loved ones in Heaven. So enjoy your life here on earth, follow your dreams and your purpose and live your life with happiness and joy and gratitude for each blessing God has given you throughout your life. There is much to enjoy on earth if we just seek the good things in life and have a great attitude in pursuing our dreams and passions. Once you are fulfilling your purpose in life you can see how wonderful life really is. Wake up each morning with a thankfulness in your heart to embrace a new day, and to go out and make each day good and glorious for you and celebrate the gift of life that God has given you, to make a difference with your life and to be a Blessing to all, and show kindness and compassion to everyone you meet. Be the difference in the world! Give of yourself to others, and you will see many rewards come back to you. There is nothing more rewarding than being a blessing in someone else's life. Uplift and inspire others to be all that they were meant to be. What a gift you would be giving to others if you did decide to do that. I believe we are all on this Universe for a reason, and I believe that reason is to be that gift to each other, to be that blessing in another person's life, and to support and give care and comfort to one another. What a great feeling it is to know that you somehow enriched the life of another person or persons!

Self care is vital to our bodies and our lives. So many people are so busy caring for others, and become so involved in all their responsibilities they sometimes forget to nurture their own selves. If we don't take care of ourselves then it is so easy to get run down and worn out doing for others. We have to find time to include "me" time, in order to feed your soul and allow rest time and to rejuvenate your body. We all need to have that space to breathe, and to allow that peace in our lives that we all need. We can get that in various ways. It can be a time to meditate, to pray, to go for a walk, spend time near a lake, time in nature or even a massage to relax your muscles in your body. I find "me" time to be vital to my life. I love going for walks and spending time outdoors. Sometimes I like to just sit on my swing on my porch and look up into the sky and take in the beauty of nature, the beautiful blue sky, the gorgeous clouds, the birds, the butterflies, the trees and the fresh air. I love taking it all in. Sometimes even sitting down and reading your favorite book can bring relaxation and peaceful time to you. Some people like to go on hikes, and that is another good way of having your private time that you need for yourself. I get my most peace through time with God.

Talking to God, praying to God, just breathing God into my life space, feeling HIS love and protection. I'm totally refreshed after my time in prayer and conversation with God.

It restores my soul! It feeds me in a unique way, feeds my spirit! What do you like to do in your "me" time? What uplifts you and gives you peace in your heart? What nurtures you in the best way? I hope you are taking time for yourself, even if it is just a short amount of time each and everyday. It will benefit you in many ways.

We all have some sort of stress that we have to deal with at times. Stress really can take a toll on the body. I've often heard that going for a walk is the greatest stress reliever there is. Taking some deep breaths and letting the stress all go to God is a big help too. I turn all my stresses to God. I just say to God, please help me God, as I do not know how to handle this. Then in my heart I know it will be taken care of and the stress leaves my body, allowing my body to have peace and my mind to relax and have peace of mind knowing full well that God is in charge and HE will take care of whatever is causing my stress. What a gift that is, to be able to "let go" of all our cares and worries, and believe in our hearts that God is in control, and rest knowing all is well!

Chapter 9

A SERVANT'S HEART

D O YOU HAVE A Servant's heart? Do you feel called in the purpose of helping others? I have always loved the idea of making someone else's life better and brighter. I believe if you give of yourself to others that you will discover the secret of real joy.

We all have been given a talent that we can share with the world. I love the concept of thinking, what can I do today to bring a blessing to someone who needs it? If I can find a way to make the lives of others better, then why not share that gift that

God has given you? There are so many little ways we can be a blessing to another person. I love the idea of the Random Act of Kindness Day. What does your soul invite you to do? It can be anything where you have an interest, such as volunteering to mow an elderly person's yard or remove snow for them. It may be volunteering at a homeless shelter or a soup kitchen, maybe even at a food pantry. We all have the perfect talent or skill to contribute to helping meet a need for others. I love to uplift and inspire people and feel that is my unique gift I have been given from

God. Where does your heart call you to serve? You have unique gifts to give also to make a difference in the lives of others. The more you focus on being a blessing to others the more wonderful blessings will come into your life. God loves a giving heart! It is really true! The more that I do for others, the more great things happen to me. There is much joy in helping another person who could benefit from your gift. What I think is important is to seek out opportunities that you would enjoy doing. It's always more enjoyable when you can choose a path of volunteering that also brings joy to you as well. Then you are not only just helping someone else but giving yourself a chance to do something you enjoy.

Do you live your life on a fast paced lifestyle, or more of a simplified life? So many families are rushing off here and there and never have time to slow down to smell the roses. Lots of activities can keep us on the go non-stop, barely having time to breathe.

It's so easy to become disconnected to our family when we are barely having enough time for ourselves. For me, I love living life simply, enjoying the daily moments of acknowledging the blessings in my life. Spending time in nature and taking in the beauty of the great outdoors and viewing the butterflies and birds as they fly about.

There is so much peace to take in when you become "still" and just listen to the sounds of the great outdoors. I have loved slowing my life down and spending my precious moments reading a great book or listening to calming music or going on a bike ride or for a walk in my neighborhood or park. AAAH, it doesn't get any better than that. The peace and tranquility of having a simplified life. Prayer time with God becomes so meaningful and enriching when we slow down and really feel the love and warmth of God all around you. The peace, joy and comfort of God! It's amazing! I used to live a pretty hectic, fast paced, lifestyle myself, always going someplace in a hurry it seemed. So much to do, so many places where my presence was needed, or so I thought. For a long time I felt so great that I had so much energy to do it all, to be a mom, a friend, a daughter and employee, and to keep on going, as the energy never seemed to stop, and was so happy that I had such motivation, and drive to keep going and so proud that I felt like I was handling it all. I even had a friend who would call me the Energizer Bunny, as I never seemed to wear down. But then one day sickness hit me hard and I was laid up with a strange virus for 13 weeks, not able to do anything for anybody, not even myself. That really threw me for a loop. My son had to come and take care of me during my illness, as I was bound to my bed, unable to walk more than a few steps. I knew I must be dying, because I was not getting well, as there was no improvement, and I was so frightened. I did not want to die! I began to pray nonstop to God to please help me, please provide healing for my body. I wanted my life back again, and I wanted to live again. It was a wakeup call that I was overdoing it, and needed to slow my life down, to simplify, and live a life more meaningful, and to breathe in the beauty of life. I noticed that my blood pressure would sky rocket when I would try to walk any distance, and would become so weak that I had to immediately get back to my bed. The days lingered on, and weeks went by. I went to doctor after doctor and no one could tell me what was wrong with me. They would do blood work on me, and tell me my blood was perfect. My blood may have been perfect, but I was far from being a healthy person. Finally, my answer came in the blink of an eye. As I had spent weeks praying to God, and then God showed up, and how thankful I was. I was laying in my bed praying as I did every day, and my arm was outstretched to the side of my bed, and all of a sudden I felt this soft breeze blow onto my arm, like an ocean breeze, and I became startled, and was asking myself where is this breeze coming from.

And THEN, The Voice came to me and said, Lalonie you are going to be fine, do not worry, you are not going to die!!! Praise the LORD! I'm not going to die, and then the voice stopped.

Those words were music to my ears, as my Lord came to me, got my attention with the soft breeze on my arm, and then spoke those amazing, magnificent words to me, and told me I'm not going to die, I am going to be fine!! Oh Wow, my life was changed instantly.

I now knew, since God told me, that I was going to live, so know longer did I have to worry and fret about my illness and if I would ever be well again. It was a Miracle!! An amazing miracle! I will never forget it as long as I live!! I did get well, and fully recovered. It did not happen overnight, it took quite some time, but I would have good days where I had energy, and then I would have bad days where I couldn't do anything.

So on the good days I would excel by enjoying those days and getting out and enjoying my life before the bad days hit again. It was like a roller coaster, the way it seemed to encircle my life, up and down, never knowing how many good days I would have until another bad day came along. But God told me, I would be fine, and I trusted and knew that indeed the day would come when I would be totally cured. And it did! 13 weeks with the virus and then I was finally completely healthy again. That illness changed my life, as I felt it was a wake up call from God, telling me I'm doing too much, running here and there and everywhere, trying to fit in so many things in my life. But in the process hurting myself, and not really living and experiencing all of God's will for my life, like the beauty of the world, the blue skies, the white lovely clouds, the moon and the stars that shined so brightly. So slow down I did. I began to only work part time and soon after started my daily process of spending time with God each and every single day, for at least an hour a day. I thanked God and praised God for the gift that HE is in my life, and spent time just talking to God, giving HIM my burdens, and feeling so loved by God and so protected. That day HE came to me in my bedroom and told me I would live, and that I will be fine and to not worry, was the day my life began to truly know in my heart that God is there for me and YOU, to bring us comfort, joy and support in our daily lives. Today I can't imagine a day without talking to God, as it brings me such joy and peace, and love and comfort. I spend my days in a simplified way, appreciating all that I have been given, enjoying the present moment of each day in thankfulness and gratitude. Really slowing down my life, stopping to smell the roses, and loving every single day I have been given, and so thankful for the gift of each new day, and truly thankful each morning that I wake up to be able to go out and be a blessing to others, to love my family, and my friends, and to make each day really count. So for me it took a major illness to open my eyes to see the beauty of each day, instead of allowing it to rush on by in the busyness of each of my days. So my gift to you is to tell you my story so you don't have to experience a major illness before you look to simplifying your life, and making whatever changes you need to make your life count and to be able to appreciate all the things in your life. It is so important to value each and every day, and each and every person in your life who are important to you.

Celebrating the gift of yourself, by being thankful for the person that you are! I am not sure if people even take the time to be celebratory of themselves, and maybe they don't even think of their birthdays as a chance to celebrate the gift of who they are, but I think it is so important to do so, because we are each full of many gifts and talents in each of our beings. So we need to celebrate the gift that we are to ourselves, to our families, to our friends, and to our jobs. Our lives are so important here on earth. God has made us in the likeness and image of HIM, and we are HIS children, and HE loves us so very much! You are a gift to the world! We each are unique individuals who are all here for a purpose. You have talents and abilities and skills to use in your lives. So always celebrate the gift of YOU and who you are, and thank God for the gift of you.

Always remember how special you are and how much you are loved! Use the gift of you to go out and make a difference in the world by being a blessing to others, and by showing love to people in your life. Realize deep down inside that you are worthy and valued and special in so many ways. You are a true gift to the world!

We all deserve to be treated with respect. That is the way we want to be treated and we need to in turn treat others with respect. Even the difficult people that are placed in our lives also deserve to be treated with respect, even though that can be challenging for us. If we can look past the challenging aspects of a person who is placed in our lives and begin to look deeper at the Christ like person that dwells inside of them. If we can do that, then we can truly treat them with respect. Dignity and Respect are words I've always loved, because no matter what, I feel each and everyone of us deserves to be treated with dignity and respect, it is our human right to expect that to be given to us. Unfortunately, many times that doesn't always happen in life. The workplace is one example that I have seen where people are being disrespected and mistreated. I have seen where bosses or supervisors talk down to their employees, and some of them go to extremes and will yell at them. How horrible that is! No one deserves that kind of treatment no matter what. The work world can be a challenging place to be, with trying to do your very best but yet there are those people who just do not know the value and the worth of kindness, dignity and respect. What do you do with people who have such little regard for others? You can walk away, and decide to not accept that behavior, and find another job, or you can stay and try treating that bully with as much kindness as possible. Sometimes if you just offer complete care and kindness to someone who is not treating you right you will quickly see another person appear to you. He or she will respond in kindly to being treated respectfully. It doesn't always work, but many times you will see a whole different part of that personality emerge, and probably one you had not seen before. So if you have an unkind person that you have to deal with, and find it difficult to deal with, and sometimes feel it's even impossible to continue in that situation, then try the kindness treatment, and see if that person responds to you in a positive way. It is so easy to run away from an aggressive person who treats you harshly, no matter how hard you try with them. But what an accomplishment it could be if you bring out the goodness in that person by your kindness approach to them, as it will help you and maybe help others that could be treated unkindly too from that person, so you would not only be helping yourself but helping others so they too would benefit from the kindness that could come from the difficult person.

Chapter 10

GRATITUDE AND THANKFULNESS

I LOVE THE WORDS GRATITUDE and Thankfulness! They bring joy to me as I contemplate all the ways in which God has given me so many blessings. Do you ever think of all that you have been given in this life? I mean, it is so amazing when you stop to think of each and everything you have in your life and how wonderfully God has

Blessed your life. The food in your refrigerator that you are able to have by the hand of God, as you are given the gift of your job that enables you to afford the food you put on your table for you and your family. The home that you live in, that God so richly blessed you with! We don't achieve things in life based on solely our abilities and talents. God gave us the abilities and talents and skills that we have so we can enjoy the fruits of our labors. I don't believe that there are any accidents or coincidences in life, as I believe with all my heart that God mapped our life journey before we were even born. From the people we meet in life, and the person we choose to marry, and even our profession and our home we live in are all a part of God's plan, and I especially believe the parents we were born to was definitely no accident. Everything happens for a reason in our lives. The people we meet in our lives are all meant to serve a purpose for us, to teach us something, or to be our lifelong friends or partners. There is a reason for the meeting of each person we encounter, all from the Grace of God. God wants us to know joy and happiness, and HE helps us create that in our own lives. Sometimes we have to take a few twists or turns to ultimately get to the real joy and the real happiness that we are destined for. I am sure you can look back at your own life's journey and see the people who meant the most to you, and see the ones who taught you some great life lessons, and see the ones who you knew that you wanted to be nothing like. Sometimes difficult people can actually teach us more than we ever thought possible. We all like to be around people who are so much like ourselves, as those are the ones where we find true friendship and enjoyment with. Sometimes it is much easier to steer clear of the challenging people we meet along life's path, as who wants to deal with conflict if we don't have to. It seems so many of us have had one parent who was loving and caring and supportive and possibly the other parent who was not so nice to us who would say hurtful things and cause pain in our lives. We love and adore the kind parent, because that parent loved you unconditionally, but the more challenging parent had conditions sometimes with their love and acceptance. So hard to relate or to even enjoy the challenging parent, so sometimes we felt pent up anger and resentment towards the difficult parent, and sometimes those emotions inside of us can last a lifetime. But when you look into the style of each parent, it is the difficult parent who may have taught us more life lessons, and may have made us stronger individuals. With the kind and caring parent all we had to do was be our loving self, we didn't have to do anything to receive the love of that parent because their love and support was forever. So we really do become who we are today based on both of our parents, as they each taught us something of value, that we are all loveable and that we are strong and capable of having all that our heart desires. It can be hurtful to have a parent who emotionally isn't there for us. What I think is important to look at though, is that they each did the best they knew how to do as our parents. Some of our parents were raised in a loving home and became loving parents to us, but some of our parents were raised in a setting where there was pain and anger and bitterness, and maybe they were even beaten down themselves by the parents who raised them. That could be why they became the challenging parent to us, they were just repeating the way they were raised.

When you can look at it like that, by really deeply searching into the depth of our parents, then we can truly see that more than anything they loved us with all of their hearts. For the challenging parent in our lives, they loved us as much as they knew how to love.

I believe when we can actually look at our parents in this way, we can finally forgive them for any wrong doing they did in our lives. Any bitterness or resentment that we have stored in our minds from the difficult parent, we can now release those feelings when we can truly understand that our parents did the very best they knew how to do.

They may not have known how to show their love for us, but that doesn't mean they didn't feel that love inside their hearts, even though they maybe couldn't express it to us. That forgiveness can sometimes take years, but once it is forgiven then it is so amazing how wonderful it makes you feel. It is like a 100 pound weight has been lifted off your shoulders. You now feel so FREE, free of the pain you endured for so many years. Once you are free of the pain, resentment, anger and bitterness, you can now look back at the good memories of your life with that difficult parent, because all the years you may have spent in agony of your vivid unhappy memories, you may have blocked out everything that was good, the times you did feel joy and happiness. When you can finally do that, then you will finally have the peace in your heart that you so much need.

So if this is you that experienced pain from a parent that was just not there for you, I pray you can now release it, so you too can have a freeing heart, and be able to be thankful to finally release your pain, and know in your heart you were loved, even if it was not shown to you due to the raising and the pain your parent may have experienced.

My daughter emailed me a beautiful poem called "Always Believe In Yourself." It is really beautiful, and I want to share it with you. It goes like this:

Always Believe in Yourself

Believe that by working
learning and achieving
you can reach your goals
and be successful

Believe in your own creativity
Believe in appreciating life
Believe in love
Believe in your dreams

I have kept this poem up on my bulletin board for the last 20 years, and I read it frequently. I believe it to be such a meaningful poem as to how we all should live our lives. Work to achieve our goals, believe in ourselves, appreciate life, have fun, love everyone in our lives and believe in our dreams. It seems like such a simple concept doesn't it? But I wonder how many of us actually do all of these things. Maybe we just need to be reminded to follow these steps on our journey. They are simple steps but yet so important, each and every one of them. Love is the most important word to keep close to our hearts, to love our family and our friends and never forget to love yourself. So remember this poem and the value of the content of each and every word, and strive to make each day count in your life. It is actually so simple when you think about it. Love life, love yourself, believe in yourself!

Chapter 11

PRAYER TIME

J ESUS AND GOD FILL my life with overwhelming joy and love! When I spend time in Prayer with God and Jesus, the one thing that always touches me so much is the magnificent feeling of love and joy that I know is coming from God and Jesus into my heart. I am overflowing with their love for me, and the tears always fall from my eyes and roll down my checks because that love is so overpowering. It truly is the strongest love I've ever felt, and it just carries me away by those feelings and emotions.

You too, would feel that overflowing love if you spent time with God, and I'm sure that those of you who do spend time, one on one, with God, know exactly what I'm talking about. There is no feeling like it in the world. We are all loved unconditionally by our

God and Jesus! They love us more than we could ever even imagine. It is so amazing to even think of the love they have for us. We are all children of God, and no matter what has happened in our lives, one thing we can know for sure, is that we are totally and amazingly loved so very much! Isn't that wonderful?

I think it is so important to always be so appreciative of everything we have in life, all the blessings that God has blessed us with. It is so beautiful to think of all the gifts we have been given by God. I believe our children and grandchildren are the most precious gifts that God has given us. The love and the joy that they bring into our lives is the best gift ever. God always has a bigger and better plan for us in our lives than we could ever imagine! So many blessings that God has given us. Our families, our friends, our church communities, and everything that brings us joy. Just waking up each and everyday and being given the gift of life on this earth to enjoy with those who are important to us. God blesses us in so many ways, and it is so important to thank God everyday for each and every blessing He has given us. Our lives did not just happen, and good things did not just occur for us, and nothing is a coincidence. Our lives are all planned out by God, so each and every happy moment we have in life, it is God we can thank for that, from the gift of our parents, to the gifts of our families and friends, homes and careers, and our very own existence on this earth. God lives in our hearts, and holds our hands and holds us in HIS love every single day! So thank HIM today for the gift that HE is to you!!

I love and adore the Lord and am so thankful for the gift that HE is to me. I cannot ever imagine my life without my prayer time with my God, as my prayer time brings so much peace and joy to my heart. It is like talking to your very best friend, as you share your day with God, and share your joys and also your sorrows, and ask and receive God's blessings into your life. You can let go of your troubles and worries to God, and know in your heart that all is well, as HE is in charge, and HE will take care of your troubles for you. I pray that if you don't have special prayer times with God, that you will start prayer time, so you too can feel the gift of God in your lives, so you can see firsthand of what I'm talking about. I pray that prayer for you!

I was in absolutely and amazing awe of Pope Francis when he came to the United States. He is a gift, and I was so glued to my TV watching for those days he was here and feeling the tremendous impact he had on the lives of the people around him in person, and those getting to take in every moment of his being. His life seems to me to be truly a replica of Jesus, as his heart goes out to the homeless and to the hungry and to the poor of the world. He gives so generously of himself to all who wish to hear him.

His words were spoken so eloquently, as people listened so intently to hear each and every word he was saying. If people would listen to him I believe it would change lives because his words seem like they are coming directly from our Jesus and our God. He really lives the life of what the Bible teaches us. I'm so thankful for the gift of him, and all the great deeds he does for our world! I pray diligently for Pope Francis that he is healthy and well, and can continue for a very long time in being such a gift and a blessing to so many who love to hear every word he speaks.

Did you know that the "light of love" from Jesus and God shines on you continually? You can trust Jesus in all times. You can think of your life as an adventure as Jesus is your constant guide and companion. Live your life close to Jesus, as HE wants a close one on one relationship with you today and always. Rest in HIS peace. Lean on HIM and trust and feel peace and completeness. HE actually designed you to live in close companionship with HIM. We, as humans on this planet Earth, will always face trouble in this life, but the most important thing is that we will always have Jesus with us to help us to handle whatever comes our way, so just know deep in your heart that Jesus is there for you every step of the way, and in troubled times turn to Jesus and ask for HIS help and guidance. HE walks with you and beside you, holding your hand and lives inside you, always there to help you and guide you in your life journey. You do need to believe in your heart that Jesus and God will help you and have trust and faith in our Lord, who is with you everyday. God loves you just the way you are. You don't have to be or do anything special to receive God's grace, as HE loves all of His children just the way they are. HE delights in providing for you, to give you joy and happiness.

Depend on Jesus for help in your lives, and praise and honor HIM always! Sit quietly with Jesus, giving HIM all your fears and worries, and know in your heart that Jesus will give you Peace in your life. Trust Jesus in every instance of your life. Jesus is with you and will watch over you always, and will be there for you, and nothing can separate you from HIS love. Jesus will Bless you in so many ways!

Always remember that you are a special person, no matter what has happened in your life, and that you are loved unconditionally and totally by our loving God, who loves you with all His heart and wants the very best for you in your life, today and always!

We all have been given spiritual gifts and divine potential. Devote yourselves to prayer and time with God to find that inner peace and joy you long for. When you are down and out, then turn your eyes to God. When life becomes hard and you become weary, turn to God and HE will restore you.

For example, I went through a bad divorce many years ago, and it left me feeling so extremely low and so distraught by all of the feelings of sadness and sorrow I was experiencing, even though I was the one to choose to leave the marriage. After I left my ex husband began experiencing heart trouble and had to be hospitalized and eventually a heart valve replacement, and for a long time I blamed myself for what he was having to live through.

I offered to help take care of him while he was recovering but he was so angry at me for leaving that he didn't want my help. Anyone that goes through a divorce experiences many difficult days ahead that can last days, weeks, months and sometimes years. But yet I knew divorce was the only option for me, as I knew I deserved a better life and so did my children. But with me now being the breadwinner of the family, and having a young son and college age daughter to feed, and provide shelter for on my low salary, I found it very challenging. But then a Miracle came for me, and this miracle was the best thing that happened to me. This miracle was named Father John Herzog, priest of St. Patrick's Catholic Church, and he offered me a job at the church as an Administrative Assistant and Bookkeeper. I felt like Father John saved my life because he brought me to God, within the presence of the church setting, performing my church tasks in my new role and found myself moving closer and closer to God. So many times in my life I feel that God has saved me!

We all have had troubles in life, as we can't escape this life without troubles and difficulties to live through. How do we get through hard times? For me, it is totally God that gets me through everything in this life. Faith is truly the answer, to have Faith in our God because when you turn to God in prayer HE will help you, as God just wants to hear from you as to how HE can help you. He wants to have the communication with you. HE wants you to lean on HIM in your time of need.

Prayer should be the most important daily event in our lives. The time you spend in prayer, takes you away from the hectic pace of everyday life. It brings you into a quiet, peaceful state of mind. God's love inspires us to be all we can be. To feel at home with God, in a life that never ends. Always accept yourself as a magnificent being, worthy of all good that life can bring. God loves you unconditionally, and HE wants your life to be full of joy, love, comfort and happiness.

A phrase I love is **"bless this home with love and laughter."** Just the thought or idea of finding ways to bless your home, and to have more love and laughter in your home is such a beautiful sentiment, as we all want love and laughter in our homes. I love the words, **"As for me and my house we will serve the Lord."** That is my favorite, as that is my motto, for me to find ways to serve the Lord, to please the Lord, to help HIS people, and I'm hoping to do that through this book. To show people through my words the importance of having Jesus and God in our daily lives, and spending time in prayer with God, so that you too can see how God will impact your lives as HE has impacted mine.

To uplift and inspire people by sharing what I've learned by having precious time with our Lord. My hope is that my words of spending time with God will give you the joy it has given me. If you start a prayer, one on one, time with God you will see for yourself how life changing your life will become. God is waiting! He wants a relationship with you so very much! With God All Things Are Possible! Believe in yourself, believe in your dreams, your wishes and hopes and desires. So I hope to shine the light on you, and to open your eyes to the wonderful world you can experience with God very much a part of your lives, by spending time with HIM in conversation and prayer. HE wants to hear what is going on in your life, what challenges you are facing, and just what would make you happy and content. He is there for YOU! Ready to listen and to help you. Of course, everything happens in God's time, not in our time, so we can't be impatient and expect immediate results when we ask for something, because that is not the way it works. God is always working behind the scenes for us, and HIS plan for your life is so much bigger than you could ever even imagine. So trust in the Lord with all your heart, lean not on your own understanding, but acknowledge HIM in all ways and know HE will direct your path. It is vital that we open our hearts to God, by doing this you can be healed of whatever needs healing in your lives. He will give you peace in your hearts. He will be your best friend in the whole world. He is listening to you always.

So go find your peace, by starting a prayer time daily with God. You will be forever grateful that you did this, as it will benefit you more than you could ever imagine. I know this through my own experience, and it is so important that you receive that message too, as I want everyone to know and experience the love from God as I have. Our life does not end when our heart stops beating, as we are all eternal and will return to God and Jesus to our eternal Home of Heaven, where we will be reunited with our loved ones. We are each on our walk to our heavenly home. We are here to walk with each other to our heavenly home. Time on earth is so short, as it goes by so quickly. We are here to learn and grow in wisdom. We are given the gift from God to come to this planet Earth, to experience life and to fulfill our purpose and our passion, to serve one another, to show kindness and to perform good deeds. It is up to each one of us as to what we will do with our lives. So I pray, that wherever you are in life, that you are living your life well and following your dreams and the desires of your heart. If not, start today in making your life great!

I happen to love Angels! I love my Guardian Angels who are with me everyday, guiding and protecting me as I go along my way. I also love the Archangels. I turn in prayer to my angels frequently. Each of the Archangels are there to help us in this life in various forms, as they each have a purpose in helping us in our lives through the areas where we have the most need. Such as:

Archangel Michael is the angel of protection, and releasing negativity in our lives.

Archangel Gabriel is the angel of learning, communication and new opportunities.

Archangel Raphael is the angel of healing, relationships, miracles, emotions & sensitivity.

Archangel Ariel is the angel of finances and weather.

So whatever is our need we can pray to that Archangel to help us along our journey. I do that often, and I feel their presence as they are there for us and they want so much to help us in our lives.

Do you have any special prayers that you are most fond of? There are many great ones. One of the ones I like is the Prayer of St. Francis. There is so much teaching in that prayer, and as students here on earth, I think we need to always continue to learn. The Prayer is as follows:

Lord, make me an instrument of thy peace.
Where there is hatred, let me sow love;
Where there is injury, pardon;
Where there is doubt, faith;

Where there is despair, hope;
Where there is darkness, light;
Where there is sadness, joy.

O divine Master, grant that I may not so much seek
To be consoled as to console, to be understood as to understand,
To be loved as to love;
For it is in giving that we receive;
It is in pardoning that we are pardoned;
It is in dying to self that we are born to eternal life.

The light of God that lives inside of you blesses you in so many ways. You can be a vision of peace in the world, and give love out into the world, as you are a child of God, the most Holy God. You can find joy and peace through the practice of prayer, and always remember to pray for one another. God is always available to you, at any time.

God is always working in your life, and you can experience the peacefulness of God within you. God wants the very best for you, as HE wants you to have happiness, good health, joy and peace. He loves you more than you will ever know. HE is your heavenly

Father, the one who loves you above all. You are blessed, in mind, body and spirit. God is always with you, every moment of your life, waiting for you to acknowledge HIM, waiting for you to talk to HIM, to share your life with HIM, and to talk to HIM about your worries, your concerns, and your burdens in this life. HE wants to help you, so give all your thoughts of concern to GOD, so HE can assist you in your needs.

It is so important to keep our focus on GOD. We are all made in the likeness and image of GOD.

Remember, GOD gives you unconditional love forever and ever. Always know in your heart that with God all things are possible!! It is so important to wake up every morning with a joyful heart, as God has allowed you to have another day on earth to go out and make a difference in your life and the lives of others merely with the presence of you and the light that shines inside of you. Love others unconditionally, without any judgements, as it is not our right to judge anyone, as we are all trying to do our best in this life. We are all brothers and sisters in Christ, as we are all connected, because we are all children of God, we are all HIS children and we are to love each other with no conditions set by us. Have positive thoughts in your mind as a negative mind never gets us anywhere. We all have things go wrong in our lives, but instead of getting upset or wanting to blame someone, always remember there are always things in our lives to feel blessed about, as others can have much worse things going on in their lives than what you are experiencing. Always know that you are guided and protected by Jesus, God and the angels, every step of the way.

Look for opportunities where you can contribute to the world by finding ways that you can share the gifts and talents that were given to you by God. Make a difference in the world. I love the phrase of, **Be The Change You Wish To See In The World**. I love those words, as there are opportunities for us all where we can be that change that we wish to see in our world, so why not go out and find ways to make this a better world, a more joyous world, a kinder world, and a world with more compassion. We all have been given gifts from God that we can share with the world. Find what that talent is that has been given to you. It is inside of you, just ready to be used and to be poured out into the world to make someone else's life much more joy filled and in return, bring many rewards to you in your own life. You are meant to have a great life! Listen to your heart for divine guidance. The love of God is with you always!

The one question I always ask myself when I'm wondering how to respond to a situation that may be uncomfortable, is that I ask myself, "what would Jesus do", and immediately I know in my heart exactly what to do or not do, what to say or not say, because I feel in my heart that I know Jesus so well, and know exactly what HIS response would be in any situation. I encourage you all to do the same, because if we react too fast or too negatively or while we may be feeling hot under the collar, then we may later regret how we responded. But if we take that moment, maybe a deep breath, and listen to our hearts and ask how would Jesus would respond in this scenario, then we may answer in a much more respectful and honorable way, a way that would be more God-like, more kind, and with more compassion. All God wants for us is to give love to all.

My Dad was the kindest, and most honorable person I ever knew. He was such a gift to me as his only daughter, and I learned so much from him, about how to live a good life, an honorable life. He was generous, thoughtful, and had much integrity. I could never say enough good things about my Dad as he was the Best of the Best! How truly fortunate I was that I was chosen to be his daughter. My Dad wrote some beautiful poetry, and I want to share with you a poem he wrote after the death of his young son, my brother, Michael Estes Bowen. The poem is as follows:

Dad's Poem

The sun had gone behind the clouds and night was drawing near.
God sent down his Angels, with tender loving care.
For HE had chosen someone to dwell around his throne.
Where temptations never enter, and sorrow is never known.
We know that he will be happy in that beautiful land so fair.
We will know that he will be watching from his beautiful home up there.
We understand but still it is hard, there is no greater cost.
For God himself gave His only son so the world would not be lost.

I am so touched by this poem, as I know my parents must have been grieving terribly, as I can feel their pain through my Dad's words in this poem. I cannot even imagine what it would be like to lose a child, as the pain must be devastating.

My great, grandfather, also was a writer, and a minister of a church, many years ago. I want to share a poem he wrote as well. It is as follows:

Sometimes Just For a Moment

By E.C. Bowen
(my great grandfather)

Sometimes just for a moment, I forget to sing His praise
And my voice sounds low and husky, and I wonder at His ways.
I forget for just a moment that my dear ones only sleep.
And my heart is filled with longing and shadows round me creep.
Sometimes my eyes seem misty for the time has seemed so long.
And I find a wistful minor cord has crept into my song.
If I stop for just a moment ere my eyes have grown so dim.
I see that all are well with them, for all live unto Him.

So close your eyes and wander far down the stream of time.
Linger at the end of a thousand years and find all things sublime.
You will find the world perfected, and the dead are raised to life.
And the earth is filled with glory and the end of pain and strife.

Yes, the dead shall be awakened, for they will hear the Master's call.
For he gave His life a ransom to redeem them from the fall.
Yes, our loved ones only sleep, with no knowledge of pain or fear.
They have only reaped the sorrow that you and I now share.
Soon they come with songs and gladness and everlasting praise.
For Him who died on Calvary to redeem them from the grave.
Then you see the smile of gladness that beams on every face.
Showing forth the Father's goodness, the Spirit given by His grace.
Then you will see that all are happy, no tears their eyes to dim.
And your loved ones clothed in beauty for all live unto him.

If sometimes you feel lonely, and your eyes fill up with tears.
Just think of the glory promised: the reign of a thousand years.
Then you will hear the glad hosannas of angels and of men
And in fancy see your loved ones now as you will see them then.
(written in 1925 by my great grandfather who was a minister)

You are amazing, just as you are. God gave you as a gift to the world, to go out and spread your sunshine and the light of Christ that lives within you. I hope you will realize what a gift you are to your community and to the world. God instilled goodness and kindness inside of you, and talent and skills, for you to make a difference in the lives of others and in your life. God lives in you! It is such a shame when we don't use the gifts and talents that God gave us, as we are a world that needs to be shown all the gifts we each have to offer. Never doubt your abilities, and always be proud of who you are, because God made you, the unique person you are, to be the gift you are to us, the world.

Love yourself, honor yourself, have confidence in the awesome person God has created you to be. We are all blessed to know you, and to see what you have to share with us.

Thank you for the gift of you, the wonderful you that you are!

The best prayer of all: John 3:16
For God So Loved the World
That HE gave HIS only Begotten Son
That Whosoever Believeth In HIM
Should not Perish
But Have Everlasting Life

That prayer says it all, as it explains how much God loves us and how HE sacrificed HIS son for us, so that we can have everlasting life. God is good, God is great, and we are loved by HIM more than we could ever even imagine. So love God back. Tell HIM how very important

HE is to you, and show HIM how thankful you are by spending time with HIM in prayer, and by showing your gratitude by honoring and praising HIM for the gift that HE is to you everyday of your life. Thank HIM for the many blessings HE has given you throughout your life, your family, friends, home, job, church, community, etc. God is the best gift of all, as HE is the Gift to each one of us, as HE never leaves our side. He is always there constantly, just waiting to hear from us, waiting for us to call out his name, waiting for us to say, help me God.

I had gotten very ill with a bacterial infection, and had gone to the doctor and he gave me a prescription for an antibiotic, so I got the prescription filled, and when I asked about side effects to the Pharmacist, he replied with, there are no side effects, but it seems many prescriptions have side effects. So when I got home I read through all the paper work that came with the prescription, which was pages of dangers listed as a potential hazard if I consume this drug, and that alone is enough to scare you to death. But what really bothered me the most was that people over 60 could be most affected by this prescription, and Yikes, that was me, I'm over 60. A mild panic set in, with me asking myself, what should I do, take a risk by taking this drug and just hoping for the best, or refraining from taking that risk and forget all about taking a chance on something that could harm me. That was the $64,000 question! What to do!! Hmmmm.

So I continued to read over all the dangers of the drug, and I kept thinking that my doctor would not have prescribed something that would intentionally harm me in any way. I Googled the drug on my computer, and it pretty much listed all the precautions as the sheets of paper that accompanied my prescription. So finally I thought, well if I want to get rid of this bacterial infection I'm going to have to take an antibiotic, so I took the plunge and opened the bottle, and took out my first huge pill, that looked like maybe it should be for horses not humans. That pill was tough going down, as it almost felt like it got stuck in my esophagus, so I kept drinking lots of water. Within one hour the symptoms began to hit me hard, at first I became so sleepy that I could hardly keep my eyes open, then I began to get so dizzy and my head was really spinning, and then when I walked I noticed how weak I was and almost unsteady on my feet. Then my brain just didn't seem to function properly, it was as though I was in a brain fog. Then the cold chills set in, and felt a fever coming on. At this point, I knew I needed to just go to bed and sleep this off, and hoped I would be all better by morning.

I quickly made it to my bed, and was thankful I didn't fall on the way to my bed. I was so relieved to be snuggled in under the covers, and hoped I would fall right to sleep which I did. But then, in the middle of the night I woke up, feeling sicker than ever, as my heart was beating fast and my breathing seemed labored, and I felt so sick all over my body, and I became so frightened as to what was happening to me, and I even began shaking uncontrollably.

I began to pray, as I knew God was there for me, and I knew HE would heal me and comfort me. I prayed non stop, repeating myself over and over, as I said, "help me Jesus, help me God, help me Blessed Mary, help me angels." I then began talking non stop to Jesus, God, Mary and the angels about what was happening to me, and asked for them to heal my body, to provide divine intervention over me, and please zap away the pill inside of me that was making me so ill. I asked them for healing, and asked that no damage would be done to my body from taking this pill, and that if there was any damage done to my liver or spleen or any organs to please restore my body to good health. I continued talking and praying and kept saying the same things over and over for probably 15 minutes or so, and then it happened....the healing began, as I could feel my body getting well and healthy again, as the sickness was leaving my body, and I was being restored by God. Oh yes, thank you God! I kept saying over and over thank you God for making me better, for hearing me, for protecting me, by not letting anything happen to me. Oh how grateful I was, and the tears began to flow, as I was so overwhelmed and filled with joy, knowing my God once again had come to my rescue in providing healing to my body.

Finally I was able to relax and fall back to sleep again as I now knew I would be fine because God made me well! Praise the Lord!! Thank God for the gift that HE is in my life! Praise the Lord for all His mercy, goodness, kindness and compassion!

This story was to show you how God has worked in my life, and how HE can work in your life too, if you only open your heart to receive God's gift and blessing to you. I could not live without my God and Jesus! He is my friend, my savior, my blessing, and oh what a blessing HE is to me. I can turn to God at any time I need to, as I know HE wants to hear from me. He wants to know about my life and how it is going, and if I have any burdens or worries, HE wants to know that too. I share everything with HIM.

A relationship with God is a great gift that you give yourself. To have God in your life and in your corner, then you have all you need!! He is there to make you well when you are sick. He is there to comfort you when you are sad. He is there to share in the joys of your life. I turn to God everyday in time and prayer and conversation, and the peace it brings into my heart is indescribable. So that is why I've written this book, to let you know what may be missing in your life, as it was in mine. Do you ever feel like something is missing in your life, and that you are on a search trying to figure out what it is? I can tell you from my experience, that search brought me to Jesus and God.

He is everything you need to live a happy and fulfilled life, at least that is what it has meant for me. My life has been changed for the better, as HE is my most precious gift.

HE is there always for me. I don't have to call him on the phone, because HE lives right inside of each one of us. HE is there to hold your hand and to embrace you. HE is waiting for you to reach out to HIM. HE loves you more than you can ever imagine, HIS love for us is the most love you could ever hope to have. We are HIS children. How blessed we are to be children of God, and to know how much we are loved. If you haven't yet reached out to God, I hope my story can help you find the way to do just that.

It truly will be a gift you give to yourself, as God is waiting, as HE wants to help you, HE wants to take away your worries and concerns you may have.

He wants to help with whatever your problem may be. God has done so much for me, blessed me many times over, and HE will do that for you, if you only reach out to give HIM the chance to do that. Please do it for you!!

You are called to live from the divine in you! People will disappoint you in this life, but God never will. God is your constant companion, always loving and caring for you and helping you along your life journey. God will never abandon you. HIS love for you is everlasting and for all eternity. God is your inner guide. Turn to God to guide you for your best way of life. The Christ light lives in each one of us and if we follow the Christ light, we will receive good things in our lives. When we turn to God in prayer, we become deeply aware of the God that lives in us. The wisdom of God is always in us and as we follow our inner guidance then great things come into our lives.

Chapter 12

INNER PEACE

TO FIND THE INNER peace we all crave, we find it in God, who lives in our hearts. By reaching out to God we then will find our peace. Stay open to the miracles of life.

Love is the most important gift we can give to ourselves and others. We have to give ourselves the care that we need, self care is vital, to love ourselves for the great gift God created in each of us. Then we are capable of giving love to others, and love is the most important gift of all to offer one another, as we are all brothers and sisters in Christ. God offers all of us love, and love is what HE wants us to give to each other too. It's the greatest gift ever! The gift of love is the greatest gift a parent can give a child. I am so grateful for the love my parents gave me. It truly is the best gift that anyone can receive from their parents. I know the love my parents gave to me has made me into the person I am today. If you receive love, then it is so much easier to give love out to others. When you do not receive love, it is hard to give that love out, because it is the gift you needed most in your life, and how do you know how to offer love if you never received it yourself. There is nothing greater than love, love from a parent, love to a child, as it makes all the difference in the world how that child will grow up and how they will see the world, and how they will treat people in their lives. I have known people who never received love as a child, and they grew up spending their whole lives in search of love, and sometimes never found it. It is a key element that we all need in our lives.

In the Bible, it says this verse, "Eye has not seen, ear has not heard, nor has it so much as dawned on man what God has prepared for those who love him." I love that verse! We cannot even imagine all the great blessings that God has in store for us. God wants the very best for us always, and HE wants us to love him too. Do you love God? Do you take time to spend time in prayer with God? HE asks so little of us, just our time to spend with HIM in prayer and thanksgiving. HE loves us unconditionally, and wants to know how Blessed we feel too, to have God in our lives. Praise and Honor is what we can give to God, to show our appreciation of HIS constant love and attention to us, that He gives to us every day of our lives. Much joy comes from time with God, as you can feel the presence of God in your heart when you do spend time talking and praying to God. He wants to hear from all of HIS children!

We are all free spiritual beings who have potential to be all that we want to be. We are children of God, the God of the Most High. You are never alone, as God is with you always! You are free to live each day with a great faith and awareness that your healer and protector is our God. God takes pleasure in hearing your prayers, so always feel free to bring all your requests to HIM. The more you pray, the more answers you can receive. God is a God of abundance. HE delights in showering blessings upon blessings to HIS children. More than anything, joy is what comes into your heart when you pray to God. You can feel that abundance of joy in your heart as you speak to God. As you open your mind and your heart to receiving God's Blessings, and spending time in prayer with God a change takes place inside of you. You become so connected to our God that the abundance of joy with your time with God is the greatest gift of all! You look forward to those times with God where you can just be yourself in honoring and praising God for His goodness, kindness, mercy and compassion that HE has for us all.

You can share with God your worries, your burdens, as you release it all to HIM, and then you can rest assured it will be taken care of, as HE always listens to our prayers.

Patience is needed when you pray to God, because the gifts from God may not always come to us immediately, as we have to wait for God to choose the right time for us to receive our gifts from HIM. Being patient in waiting for the Lord is very important.

God has blessed my life in so many ways! For example, I wanted an SUV for what seemed like such a long time. Every time I saw the vehicle of my dreams, I would wish for my dream to come true, to have a nice SUV. But I would have people say to me, oh you don't want one of those cars, the gas mileage is terrible, and it will cost you so much in gasoline, so then my desire for one would fade, for awhile, but not for long. God had provided me with a nice small car, and I did feel so blessed to have that car that took me where I needed to go, and I thanked God everyday for my small car because it was a blessing for me and a gift God had given me by providing that car for me. It was a great small car, as the maintenance on it was quite low, and I took really good care of that car.

I had my small car for 8 years, and it served me well during that time. It was not my dream car by any means, but it was a nice economical car for me and one I could afford at the time. My heart began to really yearn for an SUV once I had my small car for 8 years. But by now, I was retired, and living on a budget that I needed to stick to, so I did not see how I could afford my dream vehicle of an SUV. Then I began noticing some pretty good prices I thought for ads for small SUV's, and I was wondering if the monthly payment on that would be something that would fit into my budget. The first one I saw in the newspaper was one I really liked, but after calculating what my monthly payment would be, then I realized that payment is a little steep for me.

However, God was not going to let me give up on my dream vehicle, so He stepped into intervene and show me the way to go where I could find the perfect car for me. So then my son began an internet search for me for a Kia Soul SUV, as that is what I wanted. He found the perfect vehicle just ideal for me, and I took one look at it and fell in love with it! It was a 2011 Kia Soul SUV, only 62,000 miles, front wheel drive, 4 cylinder, great gas mileage and the color was white, it looked brand new. I even got a 6 year car loan on it, so my payment was so much better than I ever imagined it could be. I was in total shock that I could have this super nice vehicle that was an SUV, my dream car, and I could afford it in my retirement years!!! I was so overjoyed!! You have no idea how happy I was! The importance of my story, is that this blessing of this car did not come from me or my son searching for it, but that God made this happen for me, as HE brought this blessing into my life. I had been wanting this car for over a year, and actually I don't know if I ever believed I could have a vehicle like this, but God listened to my heart and my desire for this vehicle and HE made it happen, but not overnight, as I had to wait for the right time, in God's time, not my time, for this blessing to occur in my life. So this is just one example of how God wants to bless our lives, to bring us joy and happiness, as HE wants all of His children to have joy and happiness on our earthly journey. It is important to be that servant of God, and to pray to God, to honor and praise

God in our daily lives, to thank HIM for all the blessings HE brings to us each and every single day. The blessing of family, friends, our homes, our communities, our churches, our jobs, our cars, our food, our health, and so much more. God loves you more than you could ever imagine, and wants the best for you, and is there waiting to hear from you. So won't you reach out to our God and thank HIM for all that HE has blessed you with your entire life, as each gift in our lives and each blessing we have received has come from our Lord. So many wonderful things has happened to me in my life, and I owe it all to God, because HE is our true abundance, our true gift, as God is in control of our lives and wants to provide to us the desires of our heart. Open your heart up to God, not for the gifts HE will give you, because the truest gift is

God, and no finer gift could you ever have than having God in your life and in your heart because HE loves you beyond all measure. HE is your Holy Father who loves His children!! God is the one who never leaves you, as HE lives inside of you, holds your hand and embraces you with HIS everlasting love! Thank God for the gift HE is to you, and thank HIM for the many Blessings HE provides to you. Gratitude enables you to see the light of HIS presence, shining on you continually. Trust God with all your heart, all your soul, all your might and all your strength! God is the best friend you will ever have!!

I found this prayer in my Mother's belongings after she passed away, and it is a prayer all Mothers can relate to:

MOTHER'S PRAYER

Please let me keep on going Lord, from dawn to setting sun,
Till I'm no longer needed and all my work is done.
Please let me be around to see my little ones grow strong,
And keep my shoulder handy for their tears when things go wrong
Please let me make our home a place, they are happy to be in,
And help me by example to keep them free from sin.
For not until they are all prepared to face life's rocky road
Does any Mother dare to drop her burden and her load.
It is only then that she can feel, she has truly earned her rest
As thankfully she whispers, Lord, I have done my very best.....

I do love that prayer, and am sure many Mothers feel these words about their own lives, as we all want to do the best job we can as Mothers to our children.

Another prayer that is a favorite of mine, and maybe yours too, and also one I found in my Mother's possessions.

I Said A Prayer For You

I said a prayer for you today
I asked him to send treasures
Of a far more lasting kind!

I asked that He be near you
To grant you health and blessings

I asked for happiness for you
But it was for his loving care
I prayed the most of all!

So beautiful! I absolutely love that prayer, and hope you enjoy it too! I believe the best thing we can do for our families and friends is to pray for them. God is listening and does hear our prayers, so it is especially nice to pray for others as we all need prayers.

Love the Lord, with all your Heart, all your Soul, all your Might and all your Strength.

Recognize and stay aware of all the blessings God brings into your life. God is our true Gift and HE loves us unconditionally for always. We are HIS children, and HIS love for us is constant. He loves us more than we could ever imagine, and wants more for us in our lives than what we could imagine for ourselves.

I love spending time in prayer with God, where I can totally be myself, talking to God and praying to God, as HE is my best friend. He is one you can share your thoughts, your feelings, your worries, concerns and the desires of your heart. I love opening myself up to God in my daily time with HIM. He brings me joy and peace and love! It is the most special time of my day. Thanking God for all the blessings He has given us is so important, as God should be honored and praised for caring for us, for being there for us. He is the gift to us! The best gift I have received is God, and by opening my heart and mind to HIM, the more peace I have received in my heart.

Jesus and God is what we are seeking. So many times people go seeking and searching for that "more" in their life, as they feel something is missing, and that "more" they are seeking and what they are missing is our Jesus and God. When you find our Lord you will then feel like you are Home! You will then feel complete! God is our everything!

He is your prosperity, He is your Blessing, He is the one who loves you the most! All HE wants in return is your attention. HE wants a relationship with you, and you can cast your worries and concerns to Him, because HE wants to help you in your life, and wants to bring answers to make your life easier. He wants to bring you Joy and Happiness!

Ask and you shall Receive! God is waiting to hear from you. He wants you to reach out to HIM on a daily basis! He is there to help you, to heal you, to guide you and direct you to your best life! God is the answer to your dreams. He is your Holy Father! We are His children who he loves so very much! From Matthew 28:20, that verse says,

"Remember, I am with you always." Something very important to remember, because God is with you always and forever. HE lives inside of you, in your heart, so you are never without God. You can turn to HIM at any given time, as HE wants you to share your thoughts, your worries, your concerns with HIM, so HE can help you have all the joys you are so deserving of. God wants more than anything to help you in this life, because HE tells us in the Bible that there will be difficulties and challenges that we will have to face in our journey on this planet. HE wants us to lean on HIM during those tough times, and to reach out to God so HE can help us through whatever we are having to face, and HE will help us, and will ease our pain. I know this for a fact, because God has helped me through some really hard times. HE has shown me the way to overcome and brings me through whatever I am facing. I could not get through this life without the loving God that helps me in every situation! God will do that for you too, if you just reach out to HIM, and seek HIM in your life! God can and will uplift you, and give you Joy and Hope when you need it the most.

When you pray, you open yourself up to receiving Divine Guidance from our Holy Father. Your true nature is peace, love and joy. See yourself as the great creation God made you to be. You are special, unique, gifted and pleasing to our God. HE made you into the likeness of HIM. I have found that I am a better person when I am connected to God, who created me. I feel more peace and more joy in my life. God is truly the greatest gift we could ever receive! HE provides for us, and brings blessings into our lives each and everyday.

Rest in the stillness of Jesus' presence. Be still and know that HE is God. God builds bonds of trust between the two of you, as you focus on HIM, and give attention to our Lord. HE is always with you, every single moment. Worship and Praise our God each and every morning as you begin your day. It will set the tone for your day if you begin each morning worshipping and praising God because it will start your day with feeling the love of God and the Joy that HE brings to your heart. It is a gift that you give yourself when you start your day in this way.

I wrote this book to show and teach others the wisdom I have learned in spending daily time with God. It has impacted my life in more ways than I could ever explain, and I wanted each person to be uplifted and inspired in their lives the way I have, by giving myself to God in prayer and my time. I have been spending an hour or more in prayer time daily with God for the past 4 years, and I felt compelled to share this experience with as many people as possible, because I feel we all need to know that the true answers to our lives live inside of us where God

Please visit my website at www.laloniebowen.com for more information and to view my blog, my newsletter, and a link to my email address and other great information. Email me anytime at lalbw@aol.com. I would love to hear from my readers!